CONTENTS

PART 1: THE REMOTE TEAM

1.1 WHAT IS REMOTE WORK?

With the rise of new technologies and a generation that grew up in online communities, we're witnessing a shift in the way we think about work. The deviation from life-long employment to job-hopping, the opportunities of the gig economy, and the endless possibilities of digital creativity with design and coding tools were the first signs of a changing culture. In the past two decades, the internet moved into our homes and our pockets, while providing exciting new tools and experiences. When Steve Jobs pulled the first iPhone out of his pocket on a stage at San Francisco's Moscone Convention Center in 2007, we were unaware of the financial crisis still ahead of us—or what an 'app' is. Both changed the way we work today.

But before we take a deep dive into the changes our careers and professional lives are undergoing, and why the time is right to dedicate a book to it, let's take a moment to reflect on what we mean when we talk about remote work and remote teams.

Globalisation

Despite what your political view on globalisation might be, the international interconnective trade networks of today's global economy undoubtedly brought us new levels of prosperity. It has also connected people all over the world and allowed for the production of ever more complex products, created by the combined efforts of many hands.

British designer and writer Thomas Thwaites hilariously illustrated this with *'The Toaster Project'*—his 2009 attempt to build a toaster by sourcing all the raw materials, processing them, and assembling everything all by himself. He did not succeed. The result is now on display at the Victoria and Albert Museum in London, which describes the piece as *"[highlighting] the complexity of everyday mass-manufactured objects and the invisible supply chains of the globalised economy which make their low-cost production possible."*

Outsourcing

During the second half of the past century, several companies grew to become large conglomerates. Cheaper and better telecommunication made it possible to more effectively work together across large distances, and in their pursuit of expansion for the sake of economies of scale, companies realised that focusing on their core strengths would improve their efficiency. So, they began the process of *outsourcing*; removing a part of the production process or business practice to a different location. Outsourcing quickly became an opportunity for other businesses to move in and take over the production process on behalf of their client. This is still a very common strategy that provides companies with more agility to this day. Consider for example that Apple doesn't build their flagship product themselves but uses so-called 'Original Device Manufacturers' in China to build the iPhone. In marketing, it's very common for companies to hire an agency to run their campaigns.

Offshoring

As outsourcing grew in the second half of the last century, businesses figured out the benefits of relocating jobs to low wage countries. Especially blue-collar jobs like manufacturing, with automation and relatively repetitive trainable jobs; other business practises like call centres followed suit. When we talk about the relocation of jobs to another country because of the positive economic impact it has on the business, it is referred to as *offshoring*—not to be confused with 'offshore companies' that have their legal entity in a foreign country with a more favourable legal or fiscal situation. Offshoring happens when car companies decide to move their production facility from the USA to Mexico, or when a French toy factory is being closed in favour of a new factory in China.

The most important distinction between *outsourcing* and *offshoring* is that offshoring can still take place within the organisation, but always in another location, whereas outsourcing doesn't need to be in another country or state, but often takes place outside the organisation. To make this more complicated, some companies decide to practise *offshore outsourcing*, which is when both practices are combined.

When we talk about remote work, we do not refer to either of these business practices. It might make sense to the people that decided to pick up this book, but we feel that it is an important distinction to make. That doesn't mean that any of the benefits, practices, or tips on how to build and grow a successful remote team in this book are not relevant, or at least helpful to people with outsourced or offshored teams. As a matter of fact, we've spoken with many people in both situations and it occurred to us that their position has a lot in common with what we've learned. Especially in the territories of communication, company culture, and dealing with a global team in different time zones, we're sharing learnings that can help most professionals in a modern working environment.

However, when we talk about the trends and opportunities that we see for the global growth of remote work, we want to make sure we're on the same page. We will be talking about the benefits and the timing of remote work in this chapter, and they do not necessarily align with offshoring or outsourcing. With that out of the way, let's explore what else we do not consider remote work.

Regional Locations

With globalisation pushing organisations to grow ever larger with economic activities encompassing multiple countries or even continents, most organisations required a similar physical expansion. Whether it was to produce the goods they make, house the services they sold, or both; companies needed local factories and regional offices to run an international business. This comes with the same challenges as before but brings us to another point that makes remote work stand out as a different occurrence: centralisation.

Although regional locations deal with time zones, cultural differences, logistical issues, and many more challenges, they still benefit from a certain extent of centralisation. Traditional businesses with regional locations have found ways to build strong communication networks between their nodes, but often aren't truly collaborative, or at least don't need to rely on constant communication. Maybe they have a centralised accounting office that takes care of all finances, or an office managing all their operations in South Africa. The people in that office will be in the same building, taking face-to-face meetings and sharing birthday cakes. Some of the issues they face will be similar to those of remote teams, but most will not.

Freelancing and Remote Entrepreneurship

Two other phenomena are freelance work and remote entrepreneurship. They deserve a mention because some people do not recognise the legitimacy of your remote team. For people that are used to a physical office, with a staff present and ready to do their bidding, a remote team and accompanying culture has the tendency to raise questions of validity. *"Are they really your team?"* is a question you'll encounter and might have to defend more than once. The question, however, *is* valid.

With remote entrepreneurs, we're referring to people making their money with online stock trading, selling services, or setting up so-called *dropshipping* businesses and running them from a sunny location like Southeast Asia. Books like Tim Ferriss' *The 4-Hour Workweek* inspired a generation to pursue remote business ownership by becoming your own boss and balancing your time and resources. Why that was an early sign of a remote work revolution we will discuss later in this chapter.

Freelancers—and we'll include independent contractors and other self-employed people—are quite similar in the fact that they don't have an employer above them or a team below them. Some remote teams might rely on freelance workers from time to time; some remote entrepreneurs might find themself building remote teams, but as long as they don't, we'll consider them both to be self-employed. Remote work is not just about being in a different place than your clients or customers. You need to be part of a team.

Remote Teams

That leaves us with the question of what we *do* consider to be remote work. A remote team by our book (pun intended) is:

> *A team that consists of full-time members in different locations, collaborating through online communication. Some might be in the same office, but this is not the status quo.*

It is therefore not:
- An outsourced or offshore team (remote tech teams, agencies, or call

centres)
- A regional location – (multiple Tesla factories, PwC offices, or Apple stores)
- Self-employment – (dropshipping, designers, freelancers)

It is, however, possible and quite likely that we'll see more hybrid teams in the future. Consider for example a call-centre with some people working from home, or a software development team with an office and several employees in different companies.

You might already know a few people that work that way, and these roles are increasingly sought after. We've heard about Google employees taking part in video meetings because they're too busy to walk to another building for a meeting, or Amazon staff waiting 15 minutes in front of the elevators post-lunch. How many of us check our emails during our commute, work on a report at home, or pick up the phone during vacation? It begs the question, how remote are you already?

1.2 WHY/WHY NOT HAVE A REMOTE TEAM?

Now you should have a good understanding of what remote work is and what remote work isn't (at least in our view of the landscape).

We are talking about truly remote teams where you may only have one person in fifty different countries and ten time zones. This kind of company setup comes with numerous challenges, and we likely haven't experienced all of them ourselves yet. But companies with truly remote teams unlock many advantages and opportunities that would otherwise be impossible. That's the main reason we went down this path and the reason we are writing this book to empower you to do so too.

This section of the book aims to distil the scenarios, situations and circumstances where building a remote team for your company makes sense and the potential benefits that come with it. Then we'll also look at examples of companies where a remote team might not be suitable. This doesn't mean it would be impossible, but we haven't worked out how to do it!

In this chapter, I'm going to lay out some of the main reasons it's also a great option for you.

Whilst I'm predominantly talking about fully remote teams, some of the benefits certainly apply to those considering a more hybrid model.

Why have a remote team?

1. You require only a phone and/or laptop

Starting with one of the most obvious benefits of having a remote team. Pretty much the only apparatus you need to make your business a success is a laptop or computer. I've even heard of entrepreneurs running their business solely from their phones, sometimes with a Bluetooth-enabled portable keyboard.

This obviously gives you a lot of freedom! With your laptop, you can work from anywhere, have all the tools you need to manage a team and with the addition of some good headphones you are easily able to make calls or video conferences.
This is the only item you really NEED to run a remote team. Theoretically, anyone who only needs a computer to work can follow this path.

2. Save money on office space

The next easy win that many businesses will benefit from is not needing to have an office space. Office space is one of the biggest drains on finances for many companies. Primarily because it's not an investment; it's just a sunk cost. Hiring someone can enable you to make more money, but an office will rarely do that.

In San Francisco, according to Squarefoot, average asking rents for office space hover around $80 per square foot in 2020. In London, New York, and other major hubs the costs are similar, in Hong Kong, even more. If you are in a much cheaper city then this may not be so much of a burden, but the question is, is office space needed at all?

If you have a remote team you can skip this cost altogether. You may choose to invest in people's home offices or spend some money on a co-working space, but this will be a lot less than taking a lease on an office.

3. Access a bigger pool of talent

Arguably the biggest benefit of a remote team is the massive pool of talent that becomes available. This has really been a game-changer for us.

In major cities, competition is fierce for the best talent and that can make it difficult to stand out or to find who you need. In smaller towns, there may simply not be enough people to choose from to fill all of your roles with real talent.

Opening up to a remote team enables you to hire someone from nearly every country in the world. It can mean that rather than five people applying to your job ad, you might have five-hundred people applying. Some may have exceptional experience and skills that you would struggle to access at home.

It also opens your doors to workers you might not usually have access to. From parents who need flexibility, to those not living in a tech hub, to those with chronic illnesses. In fact, there is a much higher number of women in leadership roles in remote teams.

4. Leverage rare skill sets

When starting a company, you are often limited with the ideas you have and the resources you have around you to execute those ideas. One of the real beauties of remote work is that you no longer have to constrain your ideas. Maybe you are based in the US and want to sell vacations in Italy or toys in Japan or build websites for people in Saudi Arabia.

The reality is you may not speak the language, have all the skills, or the local knowledge. And you might not be able to find anyone near you that does!

A remote team gives you access to entirely new skill sets; all you have to do is find them.

5. More flexible employment decisions

Starting a new company is tough. In fact, running most small or medium companies is fraught with risk. Most businesses are interested in scaling, which often requires hiring more team members to join the mission.

Labour laws are different in every country and designed to protect any team member. I am 100% in support of this, but, depending on the country, these laws can also be very inflexible. Inflexible is not the best adjective for small businesses.

Most of your team members can be brought on on a freelance basis to work on specific projects and you are also not necessarily liable for a host of social security benefits (but we advise you compensate for that). As your business inevitably ebbs and flows, flexibility in your employment decisions and the ability to allocate capital effectively can often be hugely beneficial for growth.

6. Better utilisation of budget

The world is FULL, literally full of talent. Every time zone, country, language, skill set—there are often thousands or millions of people out there. However, finding real quality is often a challenge.

Once you open up to the whole globe for your hiring decisions you might find you can better utilise your budget. Someone in New York will demand a much higher salary than someone in most other places. Maybe you can find two highly skilled people for that same price. This doesn't mean you should pay low salaries. I'm a firm believer that you should pay-up for anyone you hire, and often in remote teams, it's still much more within budget.

You may also be able to save money on a host of services, products and other overheads that might normally come into play for your business.

7. Enables a global client base

As more and more businesses themselves go remote, the concept of buying a product or service from someone you've never met (or maybe ever will meet) becomes the norm. Video conferencing or calls are sufficient for the vast majority of client liaisons, but what can often be a stretch is if you have clients on the opposite side of the world or who maybe don't speak the same language as you.

Managing clients or requests in every time zone can start to take a strain if you are all in one place, and it's why historically SMEs (Small to Medium Enterprises) serve one market, usually the one they are in.
Opening up to a remote team allows you to easily onboard clients wherever you have a team member, localise to multiple languages to expand your target market and discover new, potentially bigger opportunities in markets you are unfamiliar with. This is the future of scaling businesses.

8. Choices over working hours and lifestyle

As a founder or an employee at a company, we are usually conditioned with a fixed schedule.

Working 9 to 5, what an inflexible way to make a living.

Many employers over the last decades have introduced offering flexible working hours, but these are still usually only semi-defined and make it unlikely you can dramatically operate outside the status quo.

Well, it's no surprise that working as part of a remote team you can have much greater flexibility about when you work. Maybe you're an early bird or prefer to have afternoons free for your family. Or maybe the opposite is true.

If you design your business, your target market, and hire to compensate for your preferred lifestyle and working hours, you can have much greater flexibility as part of a remote team.
I personally prefer to start my day later and work later. Being based in Europe, this is ideal for working with our North and South American clients, but less so for our Asian clients. So I make sure we have someone on our team who can handle that.

9. Fresh perspectives and cultural diversity

This has been one of the most unexpected and fulfilling perspectives of the whole process of building a remote team. You get to meet, work with, and talk to so many different people with different lives, cultural traditions, ways of working and viewpoints on the world.

Our team ranges from twenty years old to late forties and we have people in all of the 6 inhabitable continents. Everyone contributes a different story, perspective, and approach—and all of this together is arguably our greatest asset as a business. I love hearing the amazing anecdotes and ideas we share every single day and seeing how it impacts the team members too.

10. Make money while you sleep

There are many businesses that make money around the clock, but there are many that do not. They often operate in a single market or can only make money when their team is working.

Well, what happens if your team is always working because you have people across the globe?

That's a great situation to be in. If your working day goes from 8 hours to 24 hours, theoretically you could triple your output, triple the speed of your growth, and it means you start making money while you sleep.

11. A happier, more productive team

More reports are investigating this topic, and the results are positive. We're seeing that remote work is highly sought after and that those in remote positions are 13% more productive.

What's more, remote workers are reportedly more satisfied, leading to higher retention rates.
My experience aligns with this; hardly anyone leaves. Our team has had a 95% employee retention rate in the last year. We've had minimal issues with the team delivering the results we need for our business. Certainly, no more than a non-remote team.

12. Ability to work from anywhere

The final benefit I'd like to highlight is the ability for you yourself to work from anywhere. Digital nomading—picking up your laptop and working from a co-working space by the beach. Who doesn't like the sound of that?

If you structure your time well and get your business running like a well-oiled machine you should be able to work from anywhere you want.

We actively encourage our team to spend at least some of the year as a digital nomad. It's a great way to feel like you have way more vacation time, get inspired, and strike a good work-life balance while simultaneously growing a business.

The points I've mentioned fall under three key categories: lower expenses, increased efficiency, and a strong, global team.

Needless to say, building a remote team is not without its challenges. But with such compelling benefits, founders shouldn't be too quick to rule it out.

And yet remote teams are still relatively uncommon.

There is a huge opportunity to be ahead of the curve.

We're reaping the benefits as the founders, for the business, and for the team. Why don't you?

Why NOT Have a Remote Team?

So, I've given you twelve major benefits of having a fully remote team when compared to a centralised team. Sounds great, doesn't it?

Well, before you get too excited, I want to cover the scenarios where I believe picking a remote team might not be the best option. It's definitely a rewarding option, but it may not be suitable for every business.

1. Physical labour, selling physical goods, or requires people to be there in person

For most, this may be a little obvious. But just in case it isn't, I don't see a way to run a remote business if your business requires landscaping a garden or moving furniture. This is also probably true if you plan to open an artisanal bakery or many kinds of physical stores—like a restaurant, bar, or kindergarten.

You need people there with you to execute on your daily business activities and having someone on the other side of the globe will likely not be useful. You may be able to get some help for any digital activities, but the bulk of your workforce will have to be local.

2. Personal data, heavy business, or excessive compliance requirements

This is going to be one of the toughest businesses to run as a completely remote team. In most countries, there are heavy regulations on what can and can't be done with personal data. This could be medical records, government population information, tax data, video surveillance footage, corporate project secrets or a whole number of other areas.

Depending on the country you are in and the country of the people you want to employ, this could become a major headache for you. With it not being certain if everyone you work with is an employee (instead of a freelancer), has a highly secure way of storing data, or is from a country deemed as compliant with regulations—this is a situation I would personally advise you to avoid. A remote team may not be the best option here.

3. Immediate reactions are required

In some businesses, you require the reaction to a situation to be immediate. You can check out our chapter on time zones to see if this will help remedy the situation.

4. You are not a strong communicator

This one is more about you as a person. Are you an empathetic team leader? Are you a micromanager? Would you put extra time into onboarding? There are some specific skills suited for running a remote team. If you are not sure yet if you fit the bill, read our chapter on management to get a better idea of what is involved, so that you can make an honest decision as to whether it's for you or not.

As you can see, unless you have a specific business that can't work with a remote team, the benefits often are enormous and outweigh a lot of the cons.

So now you may have a clear idea on the benefits of building a remote team, but the question is why is the remote work revolution happening now and why should you be part of it? We'll cover that next.

◆ ◆ ◆

Words from the community

Sahin Boydas, Founder and CEO at RemoteTeams.com

My biggest advice to startups is that they should embrace remote work as the "new normal" for the future of work, and not because they just want to ride on the trend. They should pursue remote work with the mindset that they want to reduce costs, get access to a global talent pool, and create a people-first team. This will help them plan and put in place all the necessary tools, culture, and foundation needed to build successful remote companies. And to make their teams successful, they shouldn't think twice about giving trust to their employees—that's one of the most important factors in building a successful remote company.

Sara Sutton, Founder at FlexJobs and Remote.co

Remote work allows employers to create a more diverse and inclusive workplace by hiring people for whom remote work is a must-have in order to work, like people with disabilities or health issues, caregivers, military spouses, veterans, rural professionals, and others. These people may have the experience and qualifications required but simply are not able to work in an office, either part of the time or all of the time. Remote work helps employers reach them and offer meaningful employment. Remote work also helps companies hire outside their immediate geographic area, which opens them up to socio-economically diverse candidates who may not reside in the immediate area.

Darren Murph, Head of Remote at GitLab

[Having a remote team] creates added flexibility, resilience against crises, massive efficiency, and enables you to be diverse by default. Decoupling geography from results keeps a business focused on what actually matters: output.

We're at a point in time where remote isn't hamstrung by tools or technology. We have what we need, technically, to scale a global team. It simply requires leadership buy-in to hire managers of one, empower people to thrive regardless of location, and to be intentional about informal communication.

1.3 WHY NOW?

The dot-com boom in the late 1990s sparked the beginning of a technology revolution that would bring digitalisation and connectivity from universities and early adaptors to all of our homes and offices. Ever since we've seen job markets all over the world changing at an unprecedented rate.

Despite the tech bubble bursting after the turn of the century, the proverbial train had left the station and the internet was here to stay. In the early 2000s we got used to relying on the internet more and more as email replaced both fax and snail mail, Google started indexing websites on the information they shared, and students found information faster and more reliably online. Not to mention all the new forms of entertainment we gained.

Mobile Revolution

After the launch of the iPhone in 2007, Silicon Valley experienced a mobile revolution that brought connectivity and increasingly powerful computing power right into our pockets. We could listen to our music, answer phone calls, send emails, and take photos with just one device. But the most influential feature that was released the next year wasn't necessarily in the devices themselves; it was the introduction of the app store.

It was this concept that turned smartphones into a platform which allowed anyone to build new features. Most of us remember the first generation of phones and other hardware devices, which came with a fixed set of features that would only change if you'd buy a new one. Now the possibilities would only be limited to the imagination of software developers and entrepreneurs outside of Apple and Google. And, as a side effect, it created a whole new industry.

The mobile revolution gave birth to all kinds of new jobs. In an attempt to attract talent and show off their 'fun' culture, startups came up with all kinds of idiosyncratic titles like *Growth Ninja* or *Supply Chain Guru*. Silly job titles aside, thousands of people now work as iOS developers—not just a new job title—but a *job* that didn't exist a decade and a half ago. But let's look a little further and reflect on some of the technologies most of us use in our daily work environment:

- Google Maps: to navigate our commute or look for a lunch spot
- Slack; to communicate with our co-workers
- Facetime; for calls and video chat while on the move
- Google Docs; for word processing and editing collaboration
- Dropbox; to access files on multiple devices or people
- Calendly; to let people schedule a meeting without going back and forth

Most of these tools didn't exist fifteen years ago and rely heavily on mobile usage. Dropbox, for instance, was created to help people manage their files while using multiple devices, while Slack would've been severely limited if you could only use it on one device.

It's quite surprising, actually, that push notifications weren't even a feature on the first iPhones. When Apple introduced them for their iOS 3 update, they finally allowed third-party apps to tell you that you've got mail, a new WhatsApp message, Instagram like, or incoming conference call without using the app at that time. If this doesn't seem that significant, consider how often you only open an app through a notification—or how useless messaging apps would be if they can't tell you you've got a message. Even though most of us have taken notifications for granted over the past decade, they've added incredible value to our connectivity.

With the emergence of smartphones and tablets, software developers have made incredible progress connecting these devices with our (work) computers which makes the user experience almost seamless. Combined with lighter and more powerful laptops, it's now easier than ever to stay connected wherever you are.

Faster Internet, Everywhere

With mobile devices came the advances of mobile connectivity. With the exception of some developing countries, all urban areas and most rural areas now have access to fast connectivity through cable or cellular networks.

Where 15 years ago the 'internet cafe' was still a common sight in cities and travel destinations, you will now spot people on a beach in Indonesia streaming their favourite series through either the beach bar's Wi-Fi or their own 4G connection.

Though our phones have allowed us to stay connected while on the move, the prevalence of Wi-Fi in public places now also lets us connect to the internet for more productive means. More powerful, lighter laptops have replaced most of our desktop computers and the LAN cables have been replaced by equally fast wireless connections. The added benefit being that you can pick up your computer and bring it to a meeting, at home, or on a business trip. Just like most office work has gone from analogue to digital, it has now gone from stationary to mobile.

To make our connection at home or in the office possible, network operators manage the infrastructure needed to power cell towers and cable connections. They've been able to massively boost our connection speed over the past decades and are mostly responsible for the difference between our old dial-up connection and being able to live stream in 4k.

That enhanced connectivity meant it became easier to share large files. As our work became more digital and there was a need to collaborate with more people over more devices, we moved from saving files on our computers to saving them on centralized servers. Like the internet itself, your files are now accessible from any device, anywhere in the world, for everyone that's been granted access. Dropbox, Google Drive, and countless other cloud storage services work on this principle.

An interesting effect of cloud computing, which was possible because of faster connectivity, has been that it increased our data usage and as a result, we now need even faster connections. This creates a cycle where the need for better supply is followed by higher demand, which requires a better supply.

Our faster connections have also drastically improved our ability to live stream video. YouTube's success was partly because of its timing in the early 2000s, when streaming video didn't require you to download the file upfront or needed (too much) buffering any longer. Now imagine that the standard quality of those videos wasn't even close to what we have today; in 2008 YouTube increased its standard quality to 480p. Compare that to today, when we can comfortably stream 4k video, play high-resolution video games, and watch live streaming.

With today's internet speed and global accessibility, from both cable and cellular connections, reliable and high-quality video streaming is technically possible and resulted in a wide selection of tools. In addition to the technical landscape, also the user-friendliness of these tools has made big leaps and are a far cry from the early days of using Skype. Google Meet (formerly Google Hangouts), Whereby, and Zoom are a few of the many tools available today.

Email, Texting, Messaging

It's fair to say that email revolutionized professional communication. For most of us, it's now hard to imagine working in an environment where all communication goes through phone calls, snail mail, fax machines, or in person. Though email did not change the format of communication very much, it did bring us speed and convenience. In the past, companies either needed to travel or be limited to local suppliers; the alternative was to mail contracts and product samples back and forth until consensus was reached. Now, companies can email a PDF back and forth and come to an agreement before lunch. Within one generation, business communication went from weeks to hours.

The two other things that changed are the mobility of the address and scale. With email, we don't need to know where our recipients are at that moment, and we can include or invite other people into the conversation. This means we don't need to wait for the mail carrier to make their way to our office or sit next to the phone to wait for a call. Unfortunately, this also means that the lines between our professional and private lives have blurred, and clients and co-workers can find us everywhere, at any time.

But email isn't anything new. If this chapter is to tell you the times have changed and because of that we'll start seeing a future of remote work, email isn't going to convince you. But besides the fact that email has been around for a while, it did change our work life and set us up for the next step in professional communication.

For anyone who didn't grow up in the early 2000s, MSN Messenger might not have left much of an impression (or even ring a bell), but together with

ICQ, online chat rooms and a few other tools they were an early version of the social media platforms we have today. A generation grew up communicating with friends online, through instant messaging, social networks, or video games. It's no surprise that people are now used to instant communication and find it hard to settle for email any longer.

In tech startups, it has been quite common to communicate internally using HipChat, a group chat tool developed by Atlassian, or use Skype for instant messaging over the past decade. Since the launch and subsequent success of Slack in 2013, however, many more organisations replaced email with instant messaging. Slack, which also allows users to integrate 3rd party integrations or build their own, now finds itself in competition with Google and Microsoft —both of which launched similar products to jump on the bandwagon. Meanwhile, a surprisingly large number of companies use WhatsApp (formally or informally) for internal communication, while Chinese messaging giant WeChat is the go-to solution for professional communication in China.

In any case, it seems like instant messaging grew from a personal to professional communication tool and is here to stay. In retrospect it might not be so remarkable, considering how important it has become in our personal lives. Now that most businesses are switching to instant communication, complete with notifications on our mobile devices, the role of the office has become a little less significant.

Soft-where?

Another aspect of the office that has changed is the amount of software we use. Where the average 2000s' resume would proudly proclaim that the holder is proficient in Microsoft Word and Excel, today recruiters expect people to understand how to work with Asana, Google Docs, and Photoshop —let alone understand what they are.

As software became more prevalent and competitive, software developers realised that the existing distribution and revenue models didn't make sense anymore. They learned a hard lesson from the early days of the iPhone and Android app stores: they got paid once for selling their app but had to commit to ongoing costs for maintaining their app to keep it running. Not to mention the hefty fees that went to Apple and Google for setting up shop in their app stores. Software companies could improve their cash flow by selling a monthly subscription, which also makes it a lot easier for their customers to try it out first. With the 30-day free trial, the world was introduced to Software-as-a-Service (SaaS). Where you used to pay hundreds of dollars for a Photoshop license, you can now get it for less than $10—per month, that is.

Just like your files, a lot of software has since moved to cloud storage. This includes services like Spotify or Trello, which (can) run inside your browser. Project management tools like Asana or Monday don't need to be installed on your computer anymore and can thus easily be accessed remotely. This is very useful, because the files you share are not stored on your machine but are hosted on a server so your colleagues can access them if they need. Did you forget to update the status of a project you're working on? It should be no problem to update that with your laptop while you're making dinner or using the app on your phone while you're going through customs.

Better hardware and faster internet—accessible everywhere we go—allow us to use instant communication tools and other SaaS products. This puts us in a position where it doesn't really matter whether we are at the office or not. The problem is that many of these tools arrived without a real etiquette on how to use them, which can sometimes result in conflicts as the lines between our professional and our personal lives blur. Since we're online all the time, when are we at work? With so many of us answering phone calls or replying to co-workers at home and on vacation, we can turn that question around and ask: *how much remote work are you already doing?*

Cultural

English proficiency

Let's briefly consider the non-technical aspects of our connected world. The internet, our hardware, and our software made it technically possible for us to connect but does not in any way assure that we *actually* do. For that, we need to rely on another protocol: language.

Globally roughly 2 billion people speak English, and though they might not all speak it at a business proficient level, that number is growing.

International schools, exchange programs, and non-English universities offering full English programs all contribute to this as they aim to prepare students for an increasingly globalized world. From pop culture to Quora, the language of the internet age is predominantly English. A recent study by W3Techs found that over 59% of the most visited websites are in English; Russian is second with just over 8%. Despite the fact that more languages find their space on the internet as more content is being translated, young people find themselves adapting to English so they can join the conversation.

A whole generation developed an international gaze. They played online games and made friends (or enemies) all over the world. They went to international schools and stayed in touch with the people they met while travelling. And they are used to instant communication through their various devices with people that are not in the room with them.

This is the generation that is now starting their careers and will bring with them the experience of operating remotely. Balancing multiple tasks while communicating with people in a different location is nothing new to them. As a matter of fact, they might question the status quo. Why are they expected to commute, let alone move somewhere for work?

These talented, well-educated people live all over the world. They might not have the means, or even the appetite to move to places like Silicon Valley or London, and do they really need to? With the tools we now have at our disposal, maybe it's time for us to embrace the borderless nature of the internet and make remote teams work.

COVID-19

While writing this book, the world seems to have gotten a crash course in working remotely. As COVID-19 spread across the globe companies were forced to ask their teams to work from home. Although we hope that by the time you pick up this book, life has returned back to normal, it will be interesting to see what the differences are after everyone (with an office job) got to experience working remotely for a little while.

Our expectation is that although this crash course in remote collaboration will convince many companies to grant their teams some extra liberties, it will probably not have convinced most business owners that the time has come for a new kind of company. As we explained earlier, remote teams are more than just working from home, whether it is for a couple of days or a few months. The real opportunity—and challenges—are in teams that are predominantly remote and operate on a global scale.

Whether this works for you because of your global client base, or because of the options it provides you when it comes to hiring, mobility, budget, or one of the other reasons we pointed out in the previous chapter; we hope that working during the quarantine period has at least showed you that it's possible.

◆ ◆ ◆

Words from the community

Sahin Boydas, Founder & CEO at RemoteTeam.com

I see remote work doing to startups what the dot-com boom did to many internet companies. Startups that take advantage of the rise of remote work and or flexible work just like companies that took advantage of the internet, will create an easy path to success—one that they wouldn't enjoy in a brick and mortar setting. Those that fail to embrace this new work culture will find it difficult to fit in. And this will be a big factor in determining the "Amazons" or "AOLs" in the startup ecosystem in the future. Of course, just like the dot-com boom, startups would have to be careful about how they embrace remote work.

PART 2: OPERATING GLOBALLY

2.1 WORKING HOURS AND TIME ZONES

One of the great benefits of having a remote team is having people all over the world. Unfortunately, it's also the one challenge that you'll never truly overcome, and means you'll be managing wildly different time schedules. Working as an agency with international clients, this quickly became an issue during our early growth stage. Although we had enough team members on deck, we couldn't control where our clients were based, and locations between the various parties didn't always synchronise. So initially, there was a learning curve. This might be very different for your organisation; some people decide to only operate and hire within one time zone, while others look further beyond the horizon. You should ask yourself if your business would benefit from global operations, or if it's worth avoiding it despite the talent pool outside your region.

How directly relevant our experience is to you, will depend on your model, but as you build your business, consider the experiences and ultimate process we went through and hopefully skip a few of the headaches. Being efficient across multiple time zones isn't particularly difficult. It just requires getting organised and some re-thinking about how you assign your team.

Assign Time Zones

When it comes to building efficient schedules, you first need to get a solid grasp on how your team will manage multiple time zones. Admittedly, this is easier said than done. Just ask one of our US-based directors who essentially lived in the APAC time zone because his clients were based there. Did it work out for him? Well, his work got done. Was it conducive to a healthy sleep schedule? Absolutely not!

Over time, we found that dividing our team into three time zones was the most effective for strategically managing international clients. They go as follows:

1. Asia/South Pacific
2. Europe/Africa
3. The United States/South America

Each zone equates to three 8-hour shifts. But what if you're a five-person team based entirely in the US? In this case, you should try to stretch those hours as long as possible. The more coverage you can squeeze out of your continental coverage, the longer your accumulative work schedule is. That's why companies operating internationally run 24/7—some work is always getting done.

Define Work Shifts

Should your entire team work 8-hour shifts? What about 12? What's the *right* number here? The true magic behind a remote team is that working hours can really be almost anything, anywhere. These questions might help break down your company's current situation.

1. Do you provide a 24/7 service?
2. Do you have international employees with varying work hours?
3. Do you have freelancers who work when they feel like it?

Everyone reading those three questions will have a different response. The most important goal is to build a balance between your business **needs**, and what your team members can **provide**. In our case, we have several team members working in China where regulated working hours are closer to 10 hours per day. For people in the US and Europe, the workday is 8 hours. Both can live in harmony, but it's important to make sure you know what those specifications are. You'll see how having this information can help you structure your business accordingly.

Companies that offer 24/7 services also require team members working longer hours plus overtime. Do you have a structure set for overtime? Make sure you prepare for that ahead of time before hiring people. Their non-office work hours mean they will inevitably trail off what you expect are typical 9 am–5 pm shifts.

Build A Framework

You have team members spread across the globe and you've defined your time zones, now what? This is where your company's operations framework should be examined. To start, we'll break down what we encountered for the remote marketing work we've conducted for countless technology companies.

The first step was acknowledging that our team—itself based in three time zones—was originally assigned to clients spread across the entire world without unification of time zones. Yikes! This led to team members having to work late, stay up for calls in different time zones, and general grumpiness over the months that this occurred. So, we put our foot down and restructured our stakeholders by assigning them to clients in their native time zones.

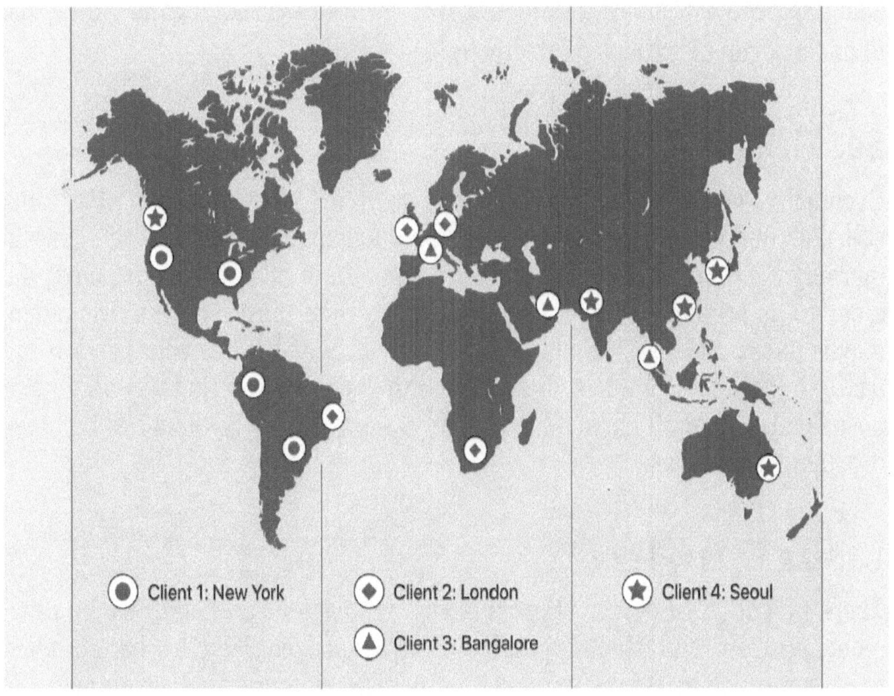

With clients in different locations, you want to assign people who have overlapping workdays.

The diagram above shows a limit of two time zones per client. We pushed to have as many team members in one time zone dedicated to a single client, but due to the job roles required for some clients, we had to stretch it. By being stricter with how we pair team members to the clients they work with, we're also improving how clients see us in return. Response times are quicker, tasks are completed in less than half the time, and employees don't have to stay up late for calls with clients on the other side of the world.

You can also consider putting some people from a more eastern time zone on a project, so your client wakes up to half a day of work already done. If you don't work with clients, this can still be good for your team as it separates the day into collaboration time and work time. Not only is the task being completed within 12 hours, but it's also giving space for other items to be addressed as well. All of a sudden you went from a busy, chaotic workspace to one that can be managed effectively.

Set Meeting Times

Eventually, you'll need to get all of your global stakeholders on the same call. For our very distributed team, we found that the optimal call time is morning Eastern Standard Time (EST). This allows other members across the globe to be present during the more pressing, time-sensitive calls. But again, maybe this is different for your delivery service where all of your vendors are based in the same continent. Just make sure that once you find a good time to host a call, you don't change it frequently—consistency is key when it comes to remote companies.

Utilize Every Tool

There's a cohort of powerful productivity applications cutting down on time, reducing stress, and keeping your company organized. Here's what our team uses day-to-day to get the job done. Of course, there are similar alternatives, but at the end of the day, just find what works best for you and stick with it. Remember, consistency is key.

Reminders – Slack Reminders

Though it requires that your team uses Slack, it is one of the most efficient tools in your wheelhouse. You can set reminders as one-time alerts or create recurring events for tasks or meetings you find yourself repeating.

Video Conferencing – Whereby

You might be wondering why we didn't put Zoom here. Something about having to launch a separate application, put in your name, create an account, and get hit with that UI just takes too much time when juggling loads of clients and team members. And what if the other person doesn't have it? Instead, Whereby gives you a unique room link. Type it into your browser and you're immediately activated and ready to go. Free rooms can hold up to 4 people with HQ video calls and paid rooms can boast 12 or more depending on the plan.

Calendar Scheduling – Calendly

Do you have clients or vendors that are constantly asking to schedule meetings with you? Jump into Calendly, create an account, and give anyone your unique link to book a call. It's filled with custom options for scheduling. The added bonus? If you're in charge of B2B outreach, it's incredibly handy to toss your Calendly link at the bottom of all outbound emails as a Call-To-Action. It shows you care and are willing to give 10 minutes of your time.

World Clock – WorldTimeBuddy

Have you ever had an event that you had to coordinate with several people across multiple time zones? Most calendars take care of this automatically by calculating the time based on where you are. If you're planning an event, however, you might want to make sure it's at a reasonable time for everyone participating. WorldTimeBuddy has helped our team line up time zones and make quick decisions.

◆ ◆ ◆

Words from the community

Sara Sutton, founder of FlexJobs and Remote.co

Some remote teams find that having core hours where everyone is available at the same time—maybe three or four hours during the day—can be helpful when working across time zones.

Another method we see used by remote teams is having one time zone for the company that everyone uses for company correspondence and planning. That way, when scheduling a meeting or an event, you're all talking about the same time zone. FlexJobs, for example, uses Mountain Time because we are based in Boulder, CO.

Managers also need to be very clear about when, where, and how teams in multiple time zones are expected to meet, communicate, and interact. Set ground rules for when to use synchronous versus asynchronous communication. Have at least one regular meeting where everyone attends simultaneously.

Liam Martin, co-founder and CMO at Time Doctor:

The main challenge is when most of the team members are in different time zones. Most teams need to be constantly collaborating to be effective and a huge time zone difference between team members can kill the collaboration.

We make sure that we have an overlapping period where everyone is working and organize meetings during these times.

We also hire people in the same time zone or where the time is only a few hours apart, especially from within one team. We use all possible ways to communicate. Video, audio, chat, email, instant messaging—all are now a part of our company's communication toolkit. Because everyone works remotely and in different time zones, our time tracking app helps us in recording what everyone is up to, and where and on what people are spending their time. We can not only spot our most productive workers but can also analyse which projects or processes are lagging and which are more profitable for our business.

2.2 PROOF-OF-WORK AND TASK MANAGEMENT

One thing that always comes up when we talk about having a remote team, is the question of how we know that people are really doing work. Like, *really*.

In simple terms, it comes down to two things:

- Good project management
- Trust

When looking at the operational side of your remote team it is very important to make sure that your team will actually get stuff done. You could argue that it starts with hiring the right people—and you'd be right—but we'll talk about that in part 3. So, let's first focus on the most important of the two: trust.

Take a Leap of Faith

While most people outside of your organisation will eventually bring up the topic of trust, they'll probably wonder how *you* can put your faith in people you've found, hired, and even paid on the internet? What's preventing this complete stranger from running with your money, stealing your business, or at the very least taking a two-hour lunch break?

Our first response to this is to turn it around. Have you ever been approached by someone online offering you money and promising they'll pay you after you put in a bunch of work? I hope you didn't jump on the occasion—unless it's a Nigerian Prince . . . I hear they're very generous. All kidding aside, when you hire someone that doesn't get to meet you in person, probably can't get a second opinion, and has little employment legislation protecting them, they are probably the one taking most of the risk. So, when it comes to trust, consider that the balance is probably lopsided.

Of course, you also need to do your due diligence. Make sure that you both commit to a contract, and an NDA if your organisation needs it. You might also want to check a reference or two if you can; though this probably depends on where your new hire is located. In addition, you should consider what security measures you should take in onboarding new hires. We'll discuss that in part 3.

But so far, we've only covered your risk. When it comes to building a remote team there is a good chance that you'll hire talent overseas, which probably means there is no legal framework to hire them as regular full-time employees and all the benefits that come with it. We had to resort to giving people freelance contracts, and this is one of the first hurdles when it comes to trust: make sure you're clear about your intentions for the employment relationship you're entering. If you consider someone a 'hired gun,' or see them as a full-time team member with whom you'd like to build a long-term relationship; make sure they're aware of it.

We've had the intention to build a team from the start, and that meant building up trust with each individual. Remember that your new hire takes a lot of risks as well, so acknowledge that and be grateful for their support. It takes both of you to take a leap of faith.

Fairness

You'll find that building trust will take longer with a remote team, but one thing that will help you is setting expectations and measuring results. The first place to start is probably payroll. Being very clear about when and how your team can expect to get paid is one of the most important aspects of your relationship with the team. Many organisations working with freelancers and remote teams think they can get away with late payments, so the people you work with might have been burned before. It goes without saying that this would be detrimental to the trust you're building. Set clear expectations with your team and take into account that international bank transfers can take a little longer to arrive.

Of course, this too goes both ways. Communicate what you expect from your team and how you expect them to do it. For example, set expectations about when they should work, how they should communicate internally and to third parties, and what your notion of remote communication etiquette is.

Goal Orientation

The work your team does depends on what industry you're operating in, but there is one thing that is universally important for remote teams: do not focus on the clock. Assuming you're not paying people to operate shifts, you're probably paying them to *accomplish* something. This is why it's important to focus more on setting goals and working towards reaching them rather than chasing people to make sure they put in their 8 hours.

When it comes to their performance, see if there is a way to quantify your team's goals. This also goes for qualitative work: even a designer can be asked to finish a set of deliverables by a deadline. As long as you pick measurable goals and agree with the team on the delivery, there shouldn't be any issues. We believe it's important to include our team in setting these goals and welcome their feedback if they think we're pushing them too much. This creates a healthy dynamic pushing the team to work hard and smart.

A goal-oriented approach will keep everyone's eyes on the prize while allowing you to keep your team accountable. If you link that to a regular meeting cycle it can be a powerful tool to keep the wind in your sails. We'll explain how to do that in a few pages.

Follow Through

It should be no surprise that when you talk the talk, you better walk the walk. Especially when it comes to trust. Pay people on time, live up to your promises and make sure you foster a culture where people can hold you accountable. This includes the promises you've made to the team and how well you can keep them. This includes the emotional aspect of the relationship you build with your team. If you'd like to evolve their trust into loyalty, make sure you've got their back and be vocal about it. Make sure that you reward individuals with incrementally more trust and accountability.

Transparency

Another way of improving the trust between you and your team is by being open and transparent about as many things as possible. Every organisation will have its boundaries but consider how far you can go. Since it's easy for individuals to feel left out in a remote team, or at least unsure about their position, it is your job to bring them back in. Being transparent about your operations, or where the team or the individual is headed can give your team a tremendous feeling of belonging and boost their confidence. Transparency is also strongly related to honesty and building a relationship on that creates a strong bond with the team as you signal that you trust them with important information.

In our experience, this is very important in a remote setting as less communication often means that signals are perceived to be more powerful. We've opened up a conversation with our team to let them know we're investing in an exciting new project that does not involve them but strengthens the organisation as a whole. By being open about this, we turned it from something they'd potentially see as an anxiety-inducing threat, into something they're proud to be a part of.

Care

Meanwhile, the most powerful way you can signal that you trust your team and would like them to place the same trust in you, is by showing empathy. It requires you and your team to be vulnerable and allow difficult conversations to occur. It also means you should take responsibility for their wellbeing.

This should apply to all organisations, but like everything we cover it is especially important to remote teams. In traditional organisations support systems often occur organically as natural leaders rise, or internal caretakers pick up the extra work. Empathy should be deeply ingrained in an organisational culture to actually work, but it starts at the centre. We don't mean that the leadership should just dictate that people should care more, but they should ask everyone what it means to be part of their team.

We found that some team members would sometimes struggle connecting on a personal level with their co-workers. After some brainstorming we decided to implement a special meeting where they could just talk about what's going on in their personal lives; we opened a Whereby room for water cooler chats; and decided to create a 'safe space' meeting without management where everyone can share how they're feeling and give anonymous feedback to the leadership.

When you hire the right people and invest in their trust, they will pay it way forward. We built a strong culture where individuals support and look after each other. The team as a whole now knows how to 'read the Zoom' and act when someone is down. We'll talk more about how to build a remote culture in section 5.

In a nutshell, remember to:

- **Take a leap of faith** – you have to *build* trust. Be vulnerable and remember your team needs to trust you as much as you need to trust them.
- **Be fair** – set expectations and measure results when you can to keep the team and yourself accountable.
- **Focus on your goal** – forget about clocking people in and focus on what you want the team to accomplish.
- **Follow through** – show that you got their back by living up to your promises and putting trust in the team.
- **Be transparent** – strengthen the relationship with your team by sharing what's going on and make them feel part of the conversation.
- **Care** – take interest in the team, emphasize with their situation, and learn to 'read the Zoom.'

Project Management

But trust only pays off when you can align your team to get stuff done. For that, you need to set yourself up for success with proper project management. As a small team, (let's say, of up to 20 people) you can probably get away without formal project management software. Good communication can make up for a lot, and like anything in this book, it will highly depend on your organisation. As you get bigger, however, this becomes a more urgent requirement.

To be honest, when we started writing this, we expected project management to be a major part of the book, good for at least a chapter or two. The good news is that if you and your team have any project management experience in the past 10 years, there's a good chance that you've moved on from analogue to digital already. Still, it might surprise you how much you still rely on good ol' flip boards and post-it notes or in-person meetings to align the team. Like anything, the key to doing this remotely is good communication.

We've been using Basecamp for most of our needs, but there are plenty of options to try out. Asana is a long-running favourite, but newer tools like Monday and even Notion have been flexing their versatility muscles. The key to picking the right tool lies somewhere in between what works best for your organisation, what works well with your other toolset, and what your team feels comfortable working with. That last part is actually very important, as a tool that doesn't work for your team gets easily neglected; potentially derailing entire projects.

Whether you hire a project manager or define one within your organisation depends on you. We've done quite well by alternating that role internally and today we are working without a full-time project manager. That's why we're making sure we've got the most effective, lightweight solutions for day-to-day task management.

Since we work with a fluctuating group of clients, we've decided to experiment a little bit with assembling teams and assigning roles and responsibilities. In remote teams, it's easy to end up eluding certain people in the organisation, especially if you live in opposite time zones or work in different departments. That's a shame, because we witnessed teams trying to reinvent the wheel and missing out on important lessons that other teams already learned. That's why we've decided to weave our client teams together as much as possible.

For each client, we assigned one team member to lead the task force and to be the point of contact. They would each get around five people to help them out with their daily tasks, but here's the twist: they would also be part of at least two other teams. These teams would each have their own team lead who is in at least two other teams. This system makes people depend on each other and realise that they can't just boss people around, or else they'll do the same thing, and nothing gets done.

Another important method to maintain structure in your projects is by implementing periodical meetings. This is hard to scale up as you grow, but you can break them down by department, location, or seniority. Just remember that it's important to remain involved with other teams as you do.

What has worked well for us has been to organise a combination of daily and weekly meetings to keep each other up to date on how things are going.

Inspired by the scrum framework, we come together during a quick daily standup to spend a couple of minutes to tell everyone:

- What you've worked on
- Where you're stuck
- What you're working on next

This simple framework allows everyone to share their accomplishments, allow people to offer their help, and offer managers a chance to adjust course before too much time has been spent on a certain task.

Standup doesn't always work with everyone depending on their time zone, so think about breaking it up into multiple standups—or even replacing it with a text version. Make sure each team member keeps it short and doesn't go into detail and be wary of two or a few people from having a conversation that doesn't benefit the group.

In addition to daily standup meetings, we get together with the whole organisation to discuss our clients on Mondays and have a weekly roundup meeting on Fridays. The Monday meeting is there to align everyone after the weekend and focus on important projects, letting mostly the team leads speak, while the Friday meetings are a weekly version of the daily standup. With a lot of people in the room, you have to be time-sensitive, so we give everyone three minutes to talk.

2.3 EFFECTIVE COMMUNICATION

Two remote workers walk into a bar. The server asks, "What would you guys like to drink?"

Remote Worker One replies, "I'm looking for something fruity, alcoholic, but not too alcoholic, using a dark spirit. I'm fine with a short or long drink."

Remote Worker Two replies, "I'm looking for a beer."

Which one of them still had a job a year later?

If this 'joke' isn't the worst you've ever heard, you need to get out more. But it does aptly describe a common internal communication problem we see with remote work: *effective communication* is the number one most important factor in the success of your remote team.

Communication problems in a remote environment become amplified and can cause rot from within which becomes very hard to shake. Whilst this is also true of any business, with a remote team, it's even harder to see the problem as it is happening. It's more difficult to sense someone's emotions if you don't hear their voice every day or see their body language. And without those watercooler conversations, you risk not getting to know your colleagues in the same way.

Repairing those problems can also be more difficult. Bad communication compounds and has an ever-growing detrimental effect on your business.

So, let's dive into some of the reasons this happens and in my experience, *what* is the best way to operate for success.

If you don't have trust, you won't have a team

When you start any job, it requires a huge amount of trust. Trust in the company, trust in the team, trust in the business, trust in the working conditions, trust that you'll get paid and, ultimately, trust in the leadership. This need for trust is amplified in a remote team, where maybe you haven't met someone face-to-face, you have less legal protection across borders, and you're further removed from day-to-day interactions.

I'd like to think that all of my team trusts me and that they know I have their back. This is much easier for team members who have been with us for one year opposed to one month. Trust is built over time. But it works both ways; you also have to trust that someone you employ is capable of doing the job, will work the amount required, and will execute the job to the standard you require.

In my opinion, building trust requires openness and honesty. If the leadership communicates this way with their team, they are more likely to receive the same treatment in return. If you build a culture of fear and stymie honest communication, then you may discourage your team's willingness to approach you with problems.

Open and honest communication is essential because it enables you to address problems as they arise, your team is much more likely to tell you about mistakes, and you can better understand the day-to-day situation your team members face.

To build trust, we strive to be approachable and reliable. We create opportunities for conversations with every team member and make those 1:1s as impactful as possible. When someone has an issue, we listen actively and quickly take steps to help. Small problems can quickly become big problems if unaddressed.

Once there is mutual trust, you can focus on growing the business and executing your strategy, removing the unknowns that eat away at people.

Commit to some core tools

As a remote team, you have to be smart about the communication tools you use. Using email as your primary communication method is likely to be too slow and lacks many functionalities, like call features or live chat. WhatsApp is another communication method that many people use in their personal lives, but messages can quickly get lost if they are more than a few days old and if a group is too big it can get overwhelming.

You must use tools that boost your ability to have efficient communication, will grow with you as your team grows, and have the functionality to suit your business.

For us, we must be able to communicate in real-time and easily separate conversations about different topics. Our tools are accessible in almost any country and they work 99.9% of the time.

We use Slack as our primary platform for communication. We use it for live chat and have separate channels for topics, projects, and non-work chats. Our other main communication tools are Whereby for conference calls, Basecamp for project management and, due to the Great Firewall, WeChat to communicate with our Chinese team. We've tried and tested at least ten of the other major options.

Everyone will have their preferences, so eventually, you have to commit to some core tools. Whatever you choose, what is essential is that it improves your ability to communicate, the majority of people see its benefits (and actively use it), and that it is affordable.
That being said, the costs of these tools are worth having. We couldn't operate effectively without most of them.

Once you get your toolkit right, it's a huge barrier you have removed from your quest for effective communication.

Don't get tripped up by time zones

Depending on just how remote and distributed your team becomes, you quickly start to run into the communication issues that arise when you have people working in different time zones, all on the same project. This is one of the only things we've found that you can't find software to magically fix!

As we've discussed earlier, the solution to this is rather more manual and mundane. Essentially it comes down to ensuring that everyone is aware of the time zones of the other people they work with. This allows everyone to structure their day and know when it's time to get the answers they need, work on a specific task or set up that important call. I know that if I want to speak to our Australian or East Asian teams, this has to be the first thing I do when I wake up. The same applies to our teams in North or South America, I can't expect an answer until much later in my day, so ideally I pre-empt this by asking the questions just before I go to bed, to allow someone to find out the answer, which I can then read the next morning.

The main skill you need to communicate across the whole globe is foresight (where possible).

- What answers or tasks do you need for tomorrow?
- Which tool is the best way to share this with your team?
- Can you give precise instructions, so that there's a high chance you get what you need the next day?
- Does the person/team need to communicate with anyone else before they can answer this and what is that extra person's time zone?

It seems simple, but I can't tell you how many times I've gotten it wrong. You are then playing time zone pinball, as a task bounces from one time zone to another around the globe, over sometimes a couple of days. Something which probably should and could have taken a couple of hours.

Effective communication across time zones is about knowing where people are when they work and giving clear instructions; and ideally, clearly enough that they don't require any follow-up questions.

Variety is the spice of life . . . and the bane of communications

Within any team, there are different styles of working and different ways of thinking. That's what makes a great team. But in a remote environment, you need to set the tone around communication.

Someone may be utterly brilliant at what they do, but if they are indecisive with their responses or struggle to give direct answers, you may have a problem. When you are all in the same time zone or office, it is often easier to go back and forth until you reach the answer you require. When it comes to a remote team, you ideally want the answer the first time because it might take 24-hours before you can get a second reply. And 24-hours can be a long time for serious issues or client problems.

Similarly, you can't presume that everything you say has been understood exactly the way you intended. Even if it seems so at the time. Of course, this applies to every workplace, but not seeing someone face-to-face, and without the chance to bump into them throughout the day and check-in, there are fewer opportunities to pick up on misunderstandings. Be direct about outcomes, and what you expect. If you leave everything too open or sounding like a question, it causes misalignment.

Varied working styles can be incredibly valuable to your business, but with remote work, too varied communication styles can spiral out of control and hinder execution. It's up to you to set the tone and set your team up for success. You can do this with company communication guidelines and backing up verbal instructions with written text.

Don't get lost in translation

One of the very best parts of having our remote team is that our members span across twenty countries. This brings different approaches, perspectives, and life experiences. We speak English as our main work communication language and my team speaks impeccable English. It's incredible just how good people can be in a second, third or even fourth language! But that makes it easy to take it for granted that everything has been understood.

The fastest way to confuse someone is by using idioms, which frankly make no sense as a literal translation. An example from British English is, "That's put a cat amongst the pigeons"—this is something I'd avoid using in a meeting because it can easily get lost in translation.

Always confirm with others around you whether or not things are clear, because sometimes people can be too nervous to ask you to repeat things. Don't overcomplicate what you are saying, speak slowly and enunciate, explaining things in the most straightforward manner, not the most poetic. This can take some practice, but it enables you to communicate efficiently with your team.

Foster organisational decisiveness

An important factor for any person leading a team is decisiveness, being able to just pick the best option and to run with it. Again, this is amplified with a remote team environment. Waiting to decide on something or not being direct with what you are looking for will likely lead to sloppy execution and unwanted outcomes.

This should be fundamental to your communication style as a remote team leader, but also something to foster in the rest of the team because ultimately you need everyone communicating efficiently for the best results.

To Summarise

As the leader of a team with remote workers, it's your responsibility to set the precedent for efficient, effective communication. Dedicate yourself to fostering a sense of trust, through openness, approachability, and reliability. And when it comes to how you communicate; I'd focus on these six main approaches:

1. **Be Clear** – with what answer or outcome you expect
2. **Be Succinct** – try to summarise everything in as fewer sentences as possible
3. **Be Direct** – don't ask if somebody would like to do something, tell them what needs to be done for speed
4. **Be Decisive** – try to choose one path to make sure your idea is executed
5. **Be Straightforward** – don't twist what you are saying. Simply outline what you need and why
6. **Be Focused** – make sure that the main point you are making stands out and that the other person will understand that

Words from the community

Øyvind Reed, CEO of Whereby

Communication is key. Teams need to be able to put more things into writing and reach out more than usual when they're working remotely. It's also really important that KPIs are clear and defined so that everyone knows what they're ultimately working towards.

Lastly, being able to strike a balance between video calls and having time to do actual work is important. Using the right tools can help with that, but then as well, it's important to use the right ones for the right problems. That sounds like a no-brainer, but so many tools are being used for things other than what they were built for.

2.4 MEETINGS

You've probably had at least one bad experience with a group call or online meeting. The sort where the energy, creativity, and very air seem to be sucked from the room. Those kinds of meetings happen when you try to treat a remote meeting exactly the same as an in-person meeting. And let's face it, a badly organised offline meeting can be just as bad.

The good news is, we've found virtual meetings to be generally more efficient. The main challenges are keeping the whole group engaged and feeling included. Of course, the fundamentals of running any offline meeting apply, as well as considerations around managing time zones and efficient communications, which we've covered in previous chapters. Therefore, here we'll focus on what we've found to be most important for running productive meetings, specific to the remote setting.

First of all, it's important to maintain a schedule of fixed meetings. This does become more difficult to manage as you grow, and will need to be adapted, but helps your team stay consistent. A general structure that works well for our team of 50 is to have Monday meetings with the whole organisation present, and team leads discussing clients. Throughout the week there are daily standups. When we started out, we had company-wide daily standups (or check-ins), but as we expanded, that became too many people to manage, so the sub-teams work on a daily basis. Fridays are for weekly roundups, a weekly version of the standups.

Setting up a Meeting

Zoom-fatigue is real. Staring at a screen isn't quite as engaging as looking around a room, and if meetings pile up, team members might not be able to give the same amount of energy. Getting the balance right is crucial, so the team doesn't get exhausted and to avoid wasting time.

It's worth considering some of these points before scheduling another meeting.

- **Does this need to be a meeting?**
  When you're remote, you really need to challenge yourself first and foremost as to whether the meeting is even needed. Whilst it's important to honour the regular weekly meetings, if it's more impromptu, consider whether an email or slack chat would suffice, or if the topics could wait until a scheduled catch up. Developing an agenda with clear outcomes and required attendees may help you decide.

- **Who needs to be there?**
  Virtual meetings tend to work better with smaller groups. So wherever possible we try to keep the numbers down. Over ten attendees, you'll have people talking over each other, or checking out mentally and not contributing at all. So, at the planning stage, think carefully about what each person can bring to the (virtual) table.

- **What time is going to work?**
  Scheduling a meeting can be tough at the best of times, and if you're working across multiple time zones it adds another level of complexity. Luckily, there are tools to help you find optimal times, such as World Time Buddy.

  If it is going to be a regular meeting, finding the right time and day is important for driving positive, inclusive discussions. If your time affects a whole time zone negatively, you might want to split it and have one to serve each group of time zones at a reasonable hour.

  Impromptu meetings can be tough to schedule with a global team, so minimising non-essential meetings keeps some space clear for last-minute calls. If you're asking your team members to be flexible occasionally that's ok, but if this happens on a regular basis, it will start to take its toll on their enthusiasm and creativity.

  Inevitably, there are times when someone has to take a call at an awkward time. When that's the case, we tend to let those people speak first, and then let them leave.

- **What's the format?**
  For regular meetings, a set structure means the team knows what to

expect so will come prepared. In our daily stand-ups, we were inspired by the scrum framework and adapted the 5-15 reporting structure for the meeting. This means short meetings to share accomplishments, areas which require support, and upcoming projects. Each attendee goes through:

- What you've worked on
- Where you're stuck
- What you're working on next

To keep on track, we limit everyone to 3 minutes.

If it's a one-off meeting, a clear agenda and measurable outcomes help develop a structure and focus. Pick someone—probably the organiser—to lead the call.

Key Guidelines for Facilitating a Meeting

We recommend you build your own manual or etiquette for meetings. The world of remote work is relatively new, and nobody has the universal truth of how to do this right. In fact, we break a few of the accepted truths when it comes to running a meeting, but here are ours for your consideration (and maybe criticism).

- **Level the playing field**
  Have you ever called into a meeting where everyone else was in the room? I suspect you ended up feeling alienated, confused or just plain bored. If some of your team are co-located, or if you're speaking with a client who is, even those team members should log in separately. This allows the rest of the group to keep track of who is on the call and who is speaking.

  Of course, the co-located callers will need to be in separate rooms, or have headphones and be muted all except one, in order to avoid feedback. If that's not going to fly with your client, ask them to at least all be on camera and to clearly introduce themselves.

- **Video off, mute on**
  This is that controversial opinion . . . Most articles you'll read on this

topic will tell you that keeping video on and mute off is essential to keeping checks on everyone on the call. As a global team, sometimes internet connection struggled with the video and sound and affected the speed and quality. Also, our team members have families or work in noisy cities, and it just helps everyone else hear the speaker. You might be picking up more background noise than you think.

There's no doubt seeing everyone is valuable—so we tend to do a few seconds at the beginning or end of a call for everyone to wave. Social, "fun" meetings are also an occasion we have video on, where possible.

You really need to try this out with your own team and see what works best for you—as a team, you might work better with videos on!

- **No interruptions**
  You'll want to set some rules of engagement; due to sound quality, we try not to interrupt each other directly and indicate that we want to talk by sending an emoji on the chat function. This skill takes a while to get used to, especially for the more enthusiastic members of the team.

- **Share materials in advance**
  When possible, sending an agenda or relevant materials in advance for a pre-read is great practice. It'll stop people being distracted during the call and will help foster discussions and empower quieter members of the team to contribute.

- **Invite small talk**
  If your team is more comfortable with each other, meetings will be far more open and productive. But remote teams have fewer chances to get to know each other on a personal level. We always start meetings with a general catch-up, going around to ask how everyone is, to make up for the casual chats in an office. Beyond meetings, you'll have to proactively create opportunities to create rapport between the team. In our fourth section on culture we'll share some of our suggestions.

- **Drive inclusion**
  Regularly going around and getting individual input, or asking specific people for their thoughts, helps everyone feel included and ensures people concentrate!

From Adjusting to Elevating

Once you've found your pace with online meetings, rather than merely surviving, you'll be able to power up the experience and actually thrive in the virtual setting.

- **Utilise tech to your advantage**
  Go beyond just adapting to online and unlock the potential of the online format. The various video conferencing platforms have different functionalities, which can be used to step your virtual meeting up a notch. For example, Zoom allows for breakout rooms, and in Whereby if someone posts a google sheet link, it can open for everyone on the call.

  In addition, there are external tools to be added. In brainstorming meetings, try polling or whiteboard tools (such as Jamboard) to make the session more interactive and creative. Sharing a screen is a good option, but we recommend you don't rely on this for too much of the meeting, as attention wanes more quickly than offline!

- **Adapt your approach in real-time**
  Even more tricky than reading the room, you've got to 'read the Zoom.' Check you're not losing anyone's attention, or if the conversation is drifting off-topic. In a remote team setting, keeping a meeting effective and focused is more important than ever. When you're not all sitting together, it's easy to lose the attention of the group.

- **Invest in equipment**
  Good equipment can be a gamechanger in the quality of your meetings. Depending on your own team meeting etiquette, you might consider investing in certain items for your team. Headsets are a great investment for improving sound, and, if you're prioritising video, a decent webcam makes all the difference. In our next chapter, we'll talk about the home office and explore this a little further.

When it comes to running successful remote meetings, a lot comes down to common (offline) meeting courtesy and solid communication skills. Ultimately, the team follows your lead, so you and your senior team should be ready to foster a collaborative and focused approach to optimise remote meetings.

◆ ◆ ◆

Words from the community

John Eckman, CEO of 10up

Meetings are pretty critical to the successful running of any agency, and being remote may make that even more true. That said, many companies don't put enough thought into what makes meetings successful. For me it boils down to: the right attendees (with where appropriate the right preparation and access to data), an agenda clearly determined in advance, and clarity about what parts of that agenda are information sharing, solution development, prioritization, or something else. If a meeting is entirely or even almost entirely information sharing, look into whether it needs to be a meeting at all, or whether the information sharing can happen ahead of the meeting so that the time in the meeting can focus on discussion, questions, and reactions to what was shared.

As a fully distributed team, we've found Zoom to be the most effective way to hold meetings with participants around the world. We have a cultural value of video-on-by-default: not to say there aren't times people need to go off camera for various reasons, but speaking to a group of faces so you can see reactions, expressions, and even just level of engagement is far preferably to speaking to a bunch of static profile photos, where you can't even tell if the person is in the room.

2.5 WORKSPACES AND THE HOME OFFICE

Where your remote team physically works is just as important as where they converge for online work meetings. As more organisations all over the world are transforming into a remote work future, there are a lot of potential implications. It might be a little early to predict a rise in English language schools in Latin America or a drop in urban real estate markets, but it's interesting to think about the role of the traditional office and how it's about to change.

During the novel coronavirus pandemic in early 2020, the world got a crash course into remote work. While for many people it was certainly not the first time they've worked from home—especially if you consider how many of us have replied to an email, answered the phone, or did a little extra work from the couch—it's a different experience to work in this environment full time. As we explained in the beginning of this book, remote teams are about breaking down the limitations of operating locally and seeing the opportunities of decentralised, fully remote teams. For starters, this means regarding the remote office not as a temporary solution, but as a permanent workplace. It's about setting expectations with your team about what their space should look like, what you can do to support a productive and healthy environment, and how as a team you can replace or even enhance old workplace traditions. In other words, get comfortable.

Workplace

The first question that comes up is where your team is actually going to work. One of the first things we did when we started building our remote team was renting office space. Yes, really. Both of our apartments didn't have a good setup for office work, so we decided to rent a space for a couple of people in a coworking space. At that time, we still expected to hire a part of our team locally, so it seemed to make sense. As we started hiring more people in different countries and built our remote team, the office became our headquarter where we've been able to spend some time with clients and team members. What we're trying to say is that the office isn't necessarily declared dead. However, it has forever been changed.

Most of the people in our team work from home, though you might come across people that prefer to work from a co-working place, or even their favourite coffee shop. One of the benefits of being part of a remote team is that it grants you more freedom to choose your workspace. Whatever their preference might be, you should think about what your expectations are from day one so you can communicate them during your hiring process. This is important because your potential new team member might have chosen to apply for a remote job because of the work-life balance it provides, and you want to agree on this before they start.

BYOD

Aside from where people work, there's the question about who supplies their hardware. In most traditional companies you'd be hard-pressed to come across a Bring Your Own Device (BYOD) policy, except for when you're dealing with freelancers. Freelancers are supposed to work with you for an undetermined or short amount of time, so setting them up with a new computer and accessories usually doesn't make sense. The issue is twofold: many remote teams have evolved from initially being a collection of freelancers, and the lack of warranty when sending expensive equipment to a stranger on the internet. We talked about trust earlier, but we've also experienced the reality of hiring people remote: it doesn't always work out. Until there is a reliable service that can take care of global procurement, distribution, and eventually the collection of equipment, this will likely remain a pain point. There are some solutions, like upgrading people's equipment over time, or giving people a budget to invest in their computer, phone, and other devices.

Another remote office characteristic is the lack of control you have over the environment that your team works in. For most team members this will probably be more of a blessing than a curse as they don't need to commute, probably feel less micromanaged or distracted. When selecting their own workspace, however, people can sometimes be unaware of the impact their environment of choice has on their work. Although we insist that their private lives are not your responsibility, you should be able to draw a line. For example, when people work from home it can be a common nuisance to be interrupted by their kids, pets, or partners. Often oblivious to this themselves, you might want to set some guidelines before it becomes a source of agitation in your team. The same applies to co-working spaces or coffee shops; your team should be responsible for a stable connection and a relatively quiet environment for calls.

This also relates to how you'd like people to present themselves in meetings; should they switch on their camera, what do you expect from their personal presentation or the space they're in? We've been pretty laissez-faire when it comes to any of these details but won't deny that many of your expectations will subconsciously seep through into your culture.

When it comes to where the office is, some of your team members might even choose to take it on the road. Some people want to work in a remote team because of the freedom of movement it gives them. The people we work with have used this advantage to see the world, be with their family, or even meet up with their remote team. You might even consider building a remote team for the same reason; we have certainly explored the options of working from another location. Our working hours are flexible—we focus on achieving results instead of input—but we do expect people to be present at meetings, be responsible for a good connection, and get the work done. Consider what you expect from your team and communicate it clearly.

We'll talk more about building a remote culture in part 4, but with the operational perspective out of the way, we wanted to share a couple of things that have helped our team deal with working from their remote office.

- **Empower your team to make their space unique to their needs.** Building a healthy and productive workspace will be unique to every one of your team members. Some want to work in dark, cool spaces with no sunlight, while others can't write a single line of code unless they can see the foliage beyond their bedroom window. If there is one thing you should take away from this chapter, it's that you need to empower them to make the best out of their office. After that, everything you provide is an add-on that will help them be more engaged in their day-to-day activities.

One way to do this is to set aside a small budget for each team member to spend on home office supplies. This can be things like a physical calendar, a USB desk fan, stress balls, or even a self-heating coffee mug. The idea is to make it clear you want them to be comfortable in their workspace, even if you can't physically be there.

- **Promote time for exercise.** Working from home shouldn't just mean 'stay inside.' It might not be the first image that pops up in everyone's mind, but exercising is an important aspect of the home office. Remind people to take enough breaks and plan some time to exercise and stay healthy.

- **Let people change their scenery.** Encourage your team to try working from a different room in their house every now and then. Working in the same home office or room can get daunting and feel like you're not getting enough stimulation. Try working from your kitchen or dining room. Small adjustments like this can make a world of difference in the long run. You can also encourage (and support) people to travel, work from a co-working space every now and then, or to come work from your office—if you still have one. We've offered people to travel to our headquarters and spend a couple of weeks with us.

Supplies & Tools

This is by no means an all-encompassing list of tools, but a good start if you're considering helping your team improve their workspace.

- **Whiteboard**
  The power of a whiteboard becomes clear the second you start using one. It might seem odd to recommend an item known for in-person collaboration, but whiteboards have helped some people on our team shift their ideas around and process their thoughts. After practising your ideas first in a couple of doodles, it might be easier to convey them to the rest of the team. Some designers choose instead to hook up an iPad so their doodles can be shared immediately.

- **Mood lighting**
  The sun is setting, your window light isn't sufficient enough, and you need to turn on an overhead light. What if it wasn't a stark fluorescent

bulb or maybe an overly yellow bulb? Being able to choose the colour hue of your workspace (especially during evening/night hours) is imperative to productivity. A few of us have the Philips Hue bulbs that put the setting in whatever mood you see fit.

- **Quality mic & headphones**
  We've all been there—12 people on a conference call and more feedback than the mic-check at a Metallica concert. This is where quality headphones and microphones do wonders. Consider that you'll all be using them at least every day, often multiple times per day. It makes sense to have that method of communication be as crisp as possible. Plus, your team will thank you big time for getting them a nice pair of headphones. The same goes for a good webcam, especially if video calls are important for you. Some people prefer to have a separate microphone; the explosion in podcast popularity has left us with plenty of consumer options.

- **Water cooler**
  I know, who but Dilbert actually uses these? A few people on our team got them and swear by the positive impact it has on their work ethic. They even set timers every hour to get up and grab a glass of water, and like reminding each other. If that's not fluidly efficient, I don't know what is.

◆ ◆ ◆

Words From The Community

Øyvind Reed, CEO of Whereby

Allowing workers to choose their own location, all the while having interesting and challenging job will significantly change how we are recruiting, employee engagement and our ability to find the best talent. The best people are no longer tied to a specific geography, but to an employer that can give them the best of two worlds. In 5-10 years the workforce will have a totally different character.

2.6 PAYMENTS AND EXPENSES

I hope this section on the practical aspects of operating globally has been enlightening. Becoming a master of time zones, execution of tasks, communicating effectively, online meetings and the home office are crucial to operating a well-oiled remote team machine. In this chapter of Operating Globally, we'll cover exactly how we go about fuelling our machine, covering everything you need to know about global payments.

It's Getting Easier

Yes, that's right, every year it gets easier and cheaper to send payments across the world. Even ten years ago, working with cross-border payments was a slow and very expensive activity. Payments might take multiple days to arrive, payments might not be possible to some countries, there might be a lot of extra paperwork with your bank and exorbitant fees that really made the whole thing less appealing for both parties.

There are now multiple options and new services launching regularly to tackle this problem. Most of the current services around remittances have focused on the retail market, so that's consumer-to-consumer transfers, for example, a family member in one country sending money to a family member in another.

Making and Receiving Payments

In the last few years, services like TransferWise, Revolut, and World Remit have started adding suitable functionality for business accounts that may come along with their own bank card and offer multi-currency bank accounts. This makes it straightforward to use the account details to send or receive payments. They also offer reasonably advanced reporting that makes it convenient when it's time to submit your accounts.

However, the main benefit of services like these is the low fees on international payments and currency conversions. To use TransferWise as an example, they allow payments in 80 currencies, allow you to set up separate bank accounts in 12 different major currencies and transfers from one currency to another can cost 10-20% of what it might cost with a traditional bank (due to exchange rate fees, transfer fees, admin fees, etc.). On average our payments sent globally might cost between $10 to $20 in fees, which may sound like a lot, but it's incredibly cheap in comparison. This allows us to work with our remote team and global client base with minimal setup or ongoing hassle. Receiving payments is also very easy and we have bank accounts, with corresponding bank details, that allow customers in many major countries to simply pay with a bank transfer. A very useful hurdle to overcome when acquiring international customers. If they can pay you like they make every other payment and either your or their fees for that are minimal, everyone wins.

With our team of fifty, that's a lot of different currencies we have to think about. But in some countries, such as China and Russia, it's near impossible to make salary payments there due to regulations and paperwork. To make or receive payments to countries that cannot be paid through the services I've outlined above, we have found the easiest way to be cryptocurrency.

If you are not familiar with cryptocurrencies this might sound a little crazy. You have probably heard of Bitcoin, but the problem with making payments in Bitcoin is that the price of one Bitcoin can fluctuate very quickly and you may think you've sent a payment of $1,000, but a day later it could be $900. This is why we strongly advise making these payments in what is called a "Stablecoin." A stablecoin is a cryptocurrency that is pegged to the value of a normal currency, mostly the dollar. This is a game-changer for fast, very low fee, cross border payments and allows you to pay anyone in the world in as little as five minutes. This then allows the receiver to convert these stablecoins into their local currency with no risk of the price fluctuating from the $1,000 you've sent.

For our business, we probably make around 50% of our payments with traditional international bank transfers and 50% with stablecoins. I believe it will become more normalised to pay cross-border payments with cryptocurrencies over the next few years. This might be a step too far out of your comfort zone right now, but the key takeaway is that new solutions are emerging all the time to tackle this issue.

When it comes to receiving payments, we also take many of our client payments in cryptocurrency. As outlined above, when using a stablecoin this allows for transfers that happen in minutes from every country in the world and we can relatively quickly turn these into money in our bank accounts if needed.

Currency Conversions

Another thing I've spent a lot of time on over the last few years is currency conversions.

Before sending any payment, I cross-reference the rate I am getting with the current rate I find on Google. You can simply Google any currency to get the live rate and equivalent amount. An example would be "1000USD in EUR" to get one thousand dollars in euros. This can be done for any currency pair including major cryptocurrencies like Bitcoin.

There are other tools and exchange rate websites, so whatever you prefer. But it is VERY important you record the exchange rate you are getting because this is likely going to be required in your accounting records and it's much easier to do something first time than going back to it all at the end of the year.

Team Expenses

For team expenses, we simply set an allowance for business trips and for other internal expenses we have a process for reporting. All payments under a certain amount (not fixed) we leave it up to the discretion of the team member to make the decision, but they must report everything on a company-wide spreadsheet. My personal opinion is that after working with me for a while, everyone on my team is capable of working out whether a $10, $20, or

$30 transaction is worth it and whether I would sanction it. So, for these kinds of amounts, I allow the team to make up their own mind and various senior team members have access to company credit cards.

Tool Expenses

It's very easy to sign up to 100 software tools. These days there's really a tool for everything you can think of. I'm a big fan of testing new tools and encouraging the team to do the same. In my opinion, this works two-fold. First is that the majority of people creating these new tools are just like you, small teams, startups trying to make something happen. They may have created something incredible and it's tough to get the mass adoption needed to create a sustainable business, so why not try them out? The second reason for testing new tools is that many teams have quite specific problems, the incumbent tool for the job might have not aged well or not be suitable for you. My belief is by testing new tools regularly you do come across some absolute gold. I've found a few tools I now use every day just because I've tested them out in the past. Spending $10 or $20 to try something out for a month can pay huge dividends long term. There is a limit where it probably starts to become unmanageable, but I don't think we are there.

It is crucial you keep track of all the tools your team is using, know how the pricing will rise over time, track whether you get locked into annual deals, what features you only unlock in the next pricing tier, etc. You should then review these tools every few months and make sure that people are still using them. As I said, it's easy to sign up and keep paying for 100 tools, but you may only be using 15 of them. The tools will make your business, but if you aren't on top of it, they can also break your business.

2.7 REMOTE MANAGEMENT

There's no doubt that managing a remote team has a whole different dynamic compared to a co-located team. Some of the best managers will struggle with adjusting to being in the room without their team, or without meeting them after work for social events. We certainly had a lot to learn—and still do. As you'll see, a lot of it comes down to those core communication skills. These traits might not come naturally to you, but just as with all skills, many can be learned and developed; so don't be disheartened.

We want to emphasise that in more ways than one, this book in its entirety should guide you to being a good remote manager. Whether it comes down to trusting people, communicating with your team, or building a remote culture; it all depends on you utilising or developing the skills you need to achieve this. Throughout these pages, we're sharing the tools we use and the frameworks we've developed, but it ultimately comes down to you to make them work. So, in addition to the operational topics that we've covered so far, we want to briefly talk about what you can bring to the table on a personal level to be successful.

EQ - Emotional intelligence

As previously mentioned in the context of communications, meeting and 'reading' your team online is more difficult than when you're face-to-face, without non-verbal cues in abundance to help you out.

Those with strong emotional intelligence are able to de-escalate conflicts, and drive productivity and motivation in the team—so there's a lot at stake.

Some ways to build your own emotional intelligence include developing your active listening skills, showing empathy and being self-reflective and self-aware. It also helps if you have taken some time to get to know the team on an individual basis.

Clarity & Brevity

Check and double-check your instructions, write them down wherever possible, write them digitally somewhere in a channel you can both see them. You're not going to bump into them at the coffee machine, and have a chat, so there's less chance to realise miscommunications.

Alongside clarity comes brevity. Being concise and accurate with what you ask someone to do is the most efficient way to communicate. If you are communicating via text (Slack, etc.) or conference call you often achieve more when you get your point across quickly, but in a friendly tone. There isn't the same amount of time as in an office environment.

Trust

Checking in every 5 minutes and asking for proof of work is only going to rile people up. There may be a short adjustment period for those new to remote work but empowering the team to make the new set up work for them will be more beneficial in the long term.

People who want to surf the internet all day were doing that already at the office! You will quickly realise it's not that different and that your team is more than capable of operating. You hired them because they are flexible and kickass.

Humour

Keep a thread or time in the calls for non-work chat, to maintain the personal bonds. It's important for everyone's sanity, but also means you remain approachable. Try to have a channel where the team can communicate about other topics or maybe even just a meme channel if that's what you are into.

Forward-thinking

As communication can sometimes be delayed (you can't just shout over the desk to someone), then you really have to master thinking ahead and setting tasks for the day, week, and month. Team members should always have an idea about what they can work on next. This is amplified in remote teams because you can't always reach someone immediately.

What it all comes down to:

Lead by example – You're setting the tone for how the team operates. Act how you'd like to see your team act.

Focus on output – If people are getting all of their work done and hitting their goals, you are also hitting your goals.

Allow time for adjustment – If you or your team have never done this before it might take some time to get into the rhythm of things.

Be thankful – Focus on some of the benefits of this set up and see it as an opportunity rather than a burden.

Words from the community

John Eckman, CEO of 10up

Most importantly, the things that make a good remote manager are the same things that make a good manager in a traditionally co-located company: sincere interest in the success and growth of the team as a whole as well as the individuals that make it up, emotional intelligence, an ability to communicate clearly and be an active listener, and an ability to understand where team members are coming from and how to work with them on their strengths and areas for improvement.

One of the cliches in our world is that people don't leave companies, they leave managers - but there is some real truth there. A huge part of any given employee's experience is going to be the individual who is their direct manager. Our annual, anonymous "heartbeat" survey includes a question about "my manager takes a clear interest in my career progression" and we find that question correlates well to overall success. That doesn't necessarily mean being best friends with all of your direct reports, but it does mean authentically engaging with them and taking an interest in their success. (Note this means not just taking that interest, but making sure that's clear to the employees - it has to be demonstrated).

PART 3: BUILDING YOUR TEAM

3.1 HIRING AND INTERVIEWS

1. Who do you need?
2. What skills are good to have for remote work?
3. Where can I find remote workers?
4. What are the characteristics of a good remote worker?

So, you've decided to take the plunge and you want to build a remote team. In the previous chapters, we've run through what a remote team is and is not, as well as a ton of advice on how to manage the operations of your team. Now we've laid the foundations, it's time to start building the house.

Like most businesses, you have probably started with a founding team or you may be a sole business owner. You might have had some success and now need to expand your team to scale. When it comes to building a team and scaling a business, you'll find hundreds of books from great founders and mega-companies. But until the last decade, practically nobody had built large-scale, remote teams, with people in every time zone and continent.

Hiring a remote team comes with its own set of challenges. Here's a quick rundown of what's different:

1. Job Search – the tools and services to find people globally just haven't been perfected yet.
2. Fitting In – even if you have hired people before, remote workers might need some different characteristics. They also may have different expectations. The lack of human contact doesn't make it any easier to integrate someone either.
3. Hiring Templates – how to find someone, what to pay them or how to train them up, can all be vastly different to your experience from where you live. Your needs are highly individualised, so even if

you find a template it may not all be relevant.

4. Regulations – the rules and regulations for hiring a remote team are likely different in every single country. Know your rights, know their rights, and make sure to protect yourself from any legal disputes.

Now that you are aware of some of the major challenges, let's look at finding you your first hire. But where do you begin?

The Remote-Hire Framework

The Remote-Hire Framework is a simple four-step process that allows you to effectively determine:

1. What are you looking for help with?
2. What seniority-level do you need?
3. What is their role?
4. If it's possible for this role to be a remote hire

We'll run through it below.

The person you need – 1 & 2

1. What are you looking for help with?

With any hiring process, this is obviously the place to start. What person do you need?
Start by listing all of the tasks you want a person to do. Ask yourself if you can find someone with all of these skills and whether one person can complete all of these tasks in a working week.

2. What seniority level do you need?

Once you have your list of tasks, start to think about what kind of skill level is needed to do these tasks, entry-level, junior, mid-level, senior or executive level. I've created a framework that can help you hire anyone, anywhere. I've given two examples below to give you an idea of what it could look like. If you've hired many people and done this process many times then you may be able to use your intuition for a lot of this, but please stick with me here.

Example One

Task	Skill Level Needed
Manage Facebook and Instagram	Junior
Create strategies for clients in Australia	Mid-level
Manage the execution of client strategies	Mid-level
Have daily calls with the team and client	Entry-level
Manage a team of 10 people	Mid-level/Senior
Create weekly reports for client	Junior/Mid-level

Example Two

Task	Skill Level Needed
Manage the recruitment process	Mid-level
Onboard new team members	Mid-level
Have weekly calls with each team member	Junior/Mid-level
Make the payroll every month	Mid-level
Manage a team of two people	Junior/Mid-level
Track vacation of an entire team	Junior

3. What is their role?

Upon having your task list and seniority level needed for each task, sometimes you might find it hard to define what a rough job title would be for this set of tasks. This is actually more important than you think, specifically for remote work. What someone is titled when they start is not so important, but when you are hiring someone, people are often looking for a certain title or expect a title to coincide with their set of skills. For example, in our business, a "Senior Marketing Manager" and "Client Services Director" could have many overlapping skills and tasks, but the people looking for these two jobs on a job board might actually have quite different work experience.

If you do not have a clear idea on what job title to give, my advice is to go to a major job board or competitors' websites. Start searching through jobs until you start to find job descriptions that sound very similar to what you need. Then if you think you have found something, look for five more jobs with that job title and if it matches, then that's probably what you are looking for.

This is going to make your job A LOT easier when you go out into the world (yes, the world) to find this person.

4. Which tasks work remotely?

From completing the task above you'll have been able to highlight the set of tasks you want someone to complete or take out of your hands. Then you've also had to think about who can perform those tasks, is this something you would expect from an intern or senior director?

Once you have made this list, now you need to think about whether or not you can hire this person remote or if you need to hire this person in a certain region. Below I've prepared two examples from the framework above to give you an idea of what might work and not work.

Example One – Senior Client Lead

Task	Skill Level Needed	Possible Remote?
Manage Facebook and Instagram	Junior	Yes

Create strategies for clients in Australia	Mid-level	Yes
Manage the execution of client strategies	Mid-level	Yes
Have daily calls with the team and client	Entry-level	Yes, but easier if closer to Australia time zone
Manage a team of 10 people	Mid-level/Senior	Yes, easiest if time zones are closer
Create weekly reports for client	Junior/Mid-level	Yes

Example Two – HR and Recruitment Manager

Task	Skill Level Needed	Possible Remote?
Manage the recruitment process	Mid-level	Yes
Onboard new team members	Mid-level	Yes, assuming reasonable time zone to the new recruits
Have weekly calls with each team member	Junior/Mid-level	Yes, assuming they are in a reasonable time zone to the other team members
Make the payroll every month	Mid-level	Yes
Manage a team of two people	Junior/Mid-level	Yes
Track vacation of the entire team	Junior	Yes

As you will see from the two examples I've used above, practically everything I would need this 'Senior Client Lead' or 'HR and Recruitment Manager' to do is possible remotely. A general rule could be that if a task or role is entirely possible on a computer or phone, then it can be done remote. But this isn't the case for everything, let me go through some examples.

Roles that might not work remote

Firstly, the biggest limiting factor to a lot of remote work is time zones. As we have stressed throughout this book, you can't beat time zones, there's no tool or software that allows you to get around it. This means there's a grey area between what is possible remote and what is undesirable to do remotely.

Speaking from experience, having a client or team member on the exact opposite side of the world (12-hour time difference) can be difficult for an extended period if you are the main point of contact. This is why having many people spread evenly across the world is advantageous. If you are a founder, you might be more likely to work strange hours, but you shouldn't demand that of your team on a regular basis (unless it actually suits them).

So if you have multiple clients in Argentina or a handful of team members in Australia, and need someone to work with groups, always think logically about where you can hire someone to create a cohesive and low-stress work environment.

Secondly, there are some roles that require people to meet up in person, attend physical meetings, events, have duties that might require them to be in a certain location or speak a certain language. I do believe that the necessity to meet in person is gradually being eroded in most roles.

As the technology for video conferencing and virtual events proliferates, we might feel the need for fewer events or for example, sales meetings happening face-to-face. But in all honesty, even as a strong purveyor of remote work, there is often a totally different energy from an in-person encounter. We'll likely see both continue but less needed and this is important when thinking about hiring.

Thirdly, this may be obvious to some, but many roles require physical work. This could be shipping for an ecommerce store, assembly of parts for a hardware product, creation of prototypes for product launch, some elements of office management or hosting physical events. If these are the sorts of tasks you are looking to hire for, you might need to consider what is possible logistically.

If you have a small office in one location and host weekly events, it may not be ideal to hire a remote events manager. It's not to say it couldn't work, but it's definitely something to factor in. This point will probably be second nature, however, to flip this on its head, the question might be, how can you make a role like this remote and not stick with the status quo?

Whatever you decide, if you have completed the **Remote-Hire Framework** you should now know:
- The tasks you want your new team member to perform
- What level of seniority you are looking for (important for salary costs)
- A potential job title
- Whether you can hire this person remotely or if you need a specific region/country

Next, let's look at how you can find that person.

Where can I find remote workers?

Jobs Platforms

A huge swathe of companies uses jobs boards to find their next hire. Simple setup, online, cheap, access to a wide range of talent. The issue with most job boards in the context of a remote team is that they are either local or national focused. That's also how most people filter them: "Jobs in Denver." Then you also have platforms like Upwork, Freelancer.com, Fiverr, etc., but these are not necessarily the best place to find people looking for a fixed job, many people prefer freelance or multiple gigs. There are plenty of career-specific job boards, for some businesses this may be enough. Then some skillsets have been remote-friendly for years, such as software development or design. If you are looking for people with these skills, there are also plenty of global alternatives. There are even sites that have a remote work focus, like FlexJobs. More and more are popping up every day.

Recruiters

If you aren't a fan of job platforms or you find yourself in the lucky position in which you can afford a recruiter, then this still doesn't mean your job search will be easier.

Side note, for anyone who's never used a recruiter before, a ballpark cost is 20% of the yearly salary of the person you hire. So, if you have a $30,000 budget for your hire, you need an additional $6,000 to pay the recruiter (again, this is a ballpark figure, there are many ways this can vary).

Most recruitment firms also think on a local or national level. Yes, there are plenty of recruitment firms who do look globally, but in my experience, this is mainly focused on executive or higher-skilled workers. Recruitment firms have their place, but I don't think they are perfect for every hire.

I believe there's going to be a huge opportunity for recruiters to take a remote-first approach over the next decade and we'll likely see many new business models spring up to serve this purpose.

Word-of-Mouth

I believe word-of-mouth is one of the best ways to find new team members, friends of friends, friends of team members, etc. Introductions from people you trust can help ease your mind and often the person who introduced would only do this if they weren't afraid of looking bad.

With our remote team, we've found this to be super useful, but the danger is that, as these scale, you can start to develop clusters in certain countries or cities. This can give you huge benefits and maybe even allow you to establish a whole branch of a business in a certain place. However, it does come with some negatives such as centralisation of labour to one time zone, potential loss of diverse perspectives and others not in clusters being marginalised.

Just be aware if you are building a cluster of friends, friends of friends, etc., and make sure you monitor how it impacts the wider company before reaching the point of no return.

Finding people to hire will always be difficult and when you look to hire globally it doesn't make it any easier, but there are great people everywhere and this extends you to a much larger talent pool. Next, we'll go through some tips of what to look for to make sure your remote hire is the right hire.

What are the characteristics of a great remote worker?

Contrary to what you might think, hiring a great remote worker isn't exactly the same as hiring a great office worker. At least from what we have found, some people have better adapted to a remote environment than others.

The lack of day-to-day visibility is one of the biggest fears for remote managers, and one of the biggest reasons all businesses haven't already moved to a remote or hybrid setup (pre-COVID-19 anyway). A few years ago, these were my biggest concerns too. But I soon found that some people really thrive in a remote setting. For us, productivity and retention rates have actually been higher in our remote team.

The reality is whether you are remote or co-located mistakes will be made, especially the first time hiring. But you soon realise what makes a good remote hire and can double-down on that archetype. Everyone has their own preferred characteristics. Here, I'm sharing my list, and the reasons for each.

Proactivity

The biggest worry for most managers hiring a remote worker is that they will be lazy and won't deliver the results you are paying for. I've found that someone who chases you constantly for the next task or even better, sets their own, is someone likely to deliver. For us, in almost every case, this has been the killer characteristic between the people we've kept and the people we let go because we believed they weren't working enough or not delivering.

Flexibility

With a global team, sometimes people may have to take a call out of working hours or move their schedule around a bit on occasion. Things can move fast and if someone refuses to budge from a strict 9-5 working schedule every single day, we might struggle to communicate or miss opportunities. It's also about mindset. Are they able to get behind a new approach or pick up someone else's work in a crisis? For me, flexibility shows understanding and a willingness to help the company progress.

Communication Skills

As we've discussed in our chapter on this topic, effective communication is the number one most important factor in the success of your remote team—and one of the biggest challenges. In a remote environment, you're often communicating over text or on a short call. Typing is up to seven times slower than talking. You need people to express opinions in an effective and efficient manner.Not to mention, not seeing someone face-to-face creates more opportunity for misunderstandings. It's more difficult to sense someone's emotions if you don't hear their voice every day or see their body language. This is why clear communication skills are important—more important than in an office setting.

Decisive Nature

Diving headfirst into a task is an attribute essential to global remote teams. If you set a task overnight for someone and it needs to be done by the next day, and often your team will need to make decisions without or when you are not online.

Therefore, you want someone who has a clear head, can make their own decisions and find their own solutions to complete the task. This is how you keep productivity high and blockages to a minimum.

Organisation and Time Management

Two things that are important to any worker, but over a distributed team in many time zones, it's essential that a person can coordinate themselves. If tasks are forgotten or people haven't been able to prioritise, then the time spent rectifying causes a domino effect.

Social and Open-minded

And finally, it's important for people to make efforts to be sociable to strengthen team relations.

One of the most valuable elements of having a remote team is in its ability to be so diverse. Our members span across twenty countries and bring different approaches, perspectives, and life experiences. But to make the most of those different walks of life, the team member needs to be open and interested in all the other ways people think and be able to collaborate effectively.

Simply saying "Good morning" every day, joining team calls, making an effort to speak to people about other topics than work; this is how you create and maintain culture.

The members of our team who contribute regularly to the non-work chats, and interact with those they don't work directly with, become the heart of the company.

It's intimidating hiring a remote worker, but if you can establish these key qualities, have a robust onboarding process and have strong communication skills in place, you can relax in the knowledge that you've done everything you can and are set for success.

How to interview for these characteristics?

It can be extremely difficult to decipher if a candidate has the skills and attitude they need for your role. As discussed above, there are certain characteristics that we look for in candidates that we believe are ideal for a remote worker. Here are some ways we try to tease out those traits in the interview process.

1) **Ask for a two-minute intro video** – we send this to all applicants with an automated email when they send in their application. In some of our earliest rounds of interviews we noticed a strong correlation between people who sent intro videos and our best team members. So, we decided to make it mandatory. Most people (including myself) don't like to make videos pitching themselves. For us, this shows someone willing to put themselves out there, put in the extra effort and it weeds out many people who are just not *that* interested in the role. You should always factor in that some people are shy, and some people might not have perfect English, but that's totally ok.

2) **Set a small project task** – this could be writing an article, making a strategy plan, small coding or design task—whatever makes sense for the role you need, a two to three-hour task. In my opinion, you should also offer to pay someone for this if it's going to take longer than an hour. The key here for me is to ask people when they can get it back to you. If people get it back to you in 24-72 hours, they probably really want the job. If people take a week or more, I have to question their commitment. Some people are very busy, but if you can't find two hours then how much do you really want this? People who promise you 48 hours and take substantially longer, are also a "No" from me. Remote work is about hitting deadlines, especially if you set them yourself! The best workers, in my experience, have always delivered

quite quickly and within the time they said they would.

3) **Book a call with them at a slightly inconvenient time** – I'm not saying book one at midnight for them, but 7 pm or 8 am could make sense. As I stress above, I wouldn't make this a habit, however, if someone point-blank refuses to ever take a call out of 9-5 to move closer to your schedule, the chances are you will run into problems at some point.

4) **Find out their ideal working schedule** – Everybody has different preferences for their working day—and being able to work non-traditional hours is a pull factor to many people moving into remote work. This can be a huge asset for the team if having more people online throughout the day is a benefit. It is very important that when you are hiring a remote team member the hours that you want them to work coincide with the hours they want to work or are willing to work. If someone wants to be a night owl and you expect them to be an early bird, then there's an opportunity for a clash of schedules. If you're a global team, taking time zones and regular team calls into account will also need to be considered. Make it clear and see what's possible.

5) **Talk through email or chat** – If you are working in an office with someone, you will likely conduct an in-person interview. I definitely recommend a video call with someone within the hiring process, but I also recommend chatting via text (email, Slack, WhatsApp, Telegram) with someone. Why? Simply because you will be doing A LOT of this going forward. Learning how someone handles text-based communication is useful to know.

6) **Ask their opinion about something** – This is pretty straightforward. Asking someone's opinion on the latest movie, the recent acquisition in your industry, the new product somebody just launched. In a remote team, opinions matter. If someone can succinctly and clearly express their opinion, then you avoid roadblocks later down the line. Indecision and long unnecessary explanations are some of the biggest time wasters when you aren't all in the same office and there's a communication delay.

7) **Talk about something other than work** – It might seem a bit of a cliché to ask someone about their hobbies. In a remote team, you should really take time to learn things like this, hobbies, interests, social lives, opinions about the world, etc. You should really try to

understand someone and more so in a remote team because you just don't get as many chances to connect. It means you have to go above and beyond to learn what makes someone tick and when better to start than in the interview.

These might sound quite different from typical interview questions like "Tell me about a time where you failed." You should definitely still ask normal interview questions! Although, it's key to think about how you determine if someone has the skills and attitude you need for your remote team. We have made many mistakes in hiring; we have also got some things right. So, my message to you is even if you've done this many times before, if it wasn't for a remote role, you might need to tweak your approach.

If you are considering building a fully remote team from day one or additionally become a hybrid remote team from a co-located one, then congratulations. I think in the next few years this will be the norm and with all the tools, experience and flexibility entrepreneurs get, they'll be a huge shift to remote-first companies. I wish you all the best.

◆ ◆ ◆

Words from the community

Darcy Boles, Director of Culture and Innovation at TaxJar

We see people get really excited about remote work, which is amazing, but that also means that remote-first/friendly companies see A LOT of applications. This can lead to not paying enough attention to candidates and also fast-tracking applicants to the role because of company growth vs. setting the right expectation, taking the time you need to hire and being OK with the process being a little slower to ensure you have the right fit for your company AND the employee.

Sara Sutton, founder of FlexJobs and Remote.co

Through interviewing more than 140 remote teams and companies at

<u>Remote.co</u>, we've learned that remote companies commonly say that they look for candidates with previous remote work experience. However, there are many candidates out there who may lack this experience but could do really well in a remote environment. So, how can you assess someone's ability to work remotely?

To address this, the hiring process should include questions and info gathering to determine whether candidates have the skills that would allow them to be a great remote worker, even without previous experience: communication skills and someone who isn't afraid to speak up, self-management, responsibility, independent work, the ability to focus, and having a growth mindset are all important.

Questions about the candidate's home office space, how they'd approach structuring their schedules and days, and what organizational and productivity methods they already use can also be helpful.

Liam Martin, co-founder of Time Doctor

Almost all our employees are fun to work with and we have achieved this by focusing on these variables that we think are really critical for hiring remotely: self-awareness, committed to mastery, passionate, self-motivated, reliable, honest, positive attitude, empathetic, good communication skills, confident, multi-tasking abilities, detail-oriented, ability to act independently (autonomy), adaptable, understand the industry, and persistence.

3.2 REMUNERATION & VACATION

You've found your dream candidate and you are ready to make them an offer. Maybe you've made job offers before, you have an expected salary in mind based on your local market, you know what perks come as standard and you know how much vacation time is expected.

But wait . . . this person comes from a country on the other side of the world, what are they expecting?

Salaries

This is the problem that hit me smack in the face the first time I started hiring people for my team. I was hiring four people at the same time, one from Australia, Pakistan, Serbia, and Canada. It was very hard for me to tell what people expected to earn.

From research on other large-scale fully remote companies, many choose to pay the "local rate." This definitely makes some sense. Paying a graduate in one country the same rate that you would pay a graduate in Silicon Valley or New York (extremely high salaries) could lead to you paying someone a salary beyond anything they would ever expect to earn. A $100,000 salary for a graduate in some countries is probably so much money, it borders on unhealthy.

Buffer has a great calculator on their website—The Buffer Transparent Salary Calculator. This is a great benchmark and starting point to see how salaries can be calculated for a new hire.

But by far the most comprehensive remote salary calculator I've seen is by the folks at GitLab. Their "Compensation Calculator" is an incredible tool that allows you to filter for role, seniority, country, and many other perks. It's open for anyone to use as part of GitLab's 3,000-page handbook. This can be a great place to start if you really have no idea, but by no means is this the only way to set salaries.

Before I knew about all of this, I had to come up with my own crude version of a salary calculator. For each role, I had a price in mind that I would pay someone in London and Berlin, London being a city with salaries nearly as high as anywhere. My personal opinion on paying salaries is there shouldn't be a huge "remote gap." Yes, some cities and countries are far cheaper to live in than others. I do believe this should be accounted for, but I don't agree entirely with paying only local rates. The way I vetted whether a salary made any sense was by researching the average salary for a doctor in that city or country. Is the rate I'm offering at all logical? This was with my very crude assumption that being a doctor is a well-paid reasonably comfortable income globally. I am not recommending this method, but it helped me get some context in the early days.

For some people, a major upside of building a remote team is the potential cost savings through salaries. But much like with any pay gap, I don't think you should just pay someone a lower rate because you can. I like to pay my team either what they would expect to earn or above. Why? Because, as a company, I believe that we should have some element of equality across the board. It's not an exact science and there are many variables, but I feel for the culture it's always good to pay people equally and we factor in a small discount dependent on the location.

Whatever method you decide to go with, being transparent and fair is the best way to build trust.

Paid Vacation and Public Holidays

This has been fascinating to both learn about and also come up with a policy. If you aren't aware, paid vacation days vary massively across the world. In the US, the consensus seems to be around ten workdays (two workweeks) paid vacation a year. In Europe, you can sometimes expect up to thirty workdays (six workweeks). In China, it is customary to have a full week off for both Chinese New Year and Golden Week, where practically everything is shut down and people travel from the big city back to their families.

With such disparities, it isn't always straightforward to set a policy that works for everyone. The other major factor in this decision for us has been the nature of our business. We have clients across the globe and just because it's a public holiday in one country, it might not be in the countries where our clients are. Trust me, it is very hard to track all public holidays in the twenty countries we have team members and hope that allowing all of them wouldn't impact our business.

The way we have approached this is two-fold. In Germany (where I'm based), the standard is to allow twenty workdays (four workweeks) per year. As we feel this is a healthy amount, we give this to everyone globally. For Americans expecting ten days, it was a bit of a shock! We try our best to make sure everyone takes these vacation days because it's good for business if people are healthy and have enough time for themselves.

With public holidays, we created our own format. Public holidays are often an important time to celebrate a religious holiday, meet with family or remember an important time in your country's history. If you miss every single public holiday due to work commitments, you often miss some of the best opportunities to see family and friends. In Europe and the US, Christmas is the staple public holiday time of year, conveniently corresponding to the year-end and logical breakpoint. But unsurprisingly, many countries don't celebrate Christmas at all. For many, New Year's Eve is a huge event and we've learned that Russians celebrate Orthodox Christmas in early January. Because of these different events, we are practically a 24/7, 365 day a year company.

Our policy for public holidays is that everyone can choose any five days to take that best suits them and what they want to celebrate. It could be Christmas, Eid, Diwali, or Passover; it's important to respect where everyone is from and build that into your business. Our only exception to this rule is China, who get two weeks' worth of public holidays (as mentioned above) and the corresponding reduction in vacation days.

3.3 ONBOARDING

When you've decided to build your remote team and have a strategy in mind for how to hire the right people, it's time to think about the operational differences between remote teams and centralised organisations. Whether it comes down to communication, meetings, or any of the other things we've discussed in part 2; you're going to want to prepare your new team members for their new remote workplace.

If you're lucky, or if you decided to look for it specifically, your new team member is already used to being part of a remote team. Congrats! But regardless of past experience, it is still a good idea to start with a fresh look at what it means to be part of a remote team, and most importantly, explain what it means in *your* organisation.

To do this effectively you should spend some time thinking about your onboarding process. Like many of the other things we've discussed in this book, it's easy to approach remote onboarding 'the same, but online.' Neglecting this process, however, means you could set yourself and your team up for failure as unspoken expectations fail to be communicated. You might have certain expectations about behaviour, communication, and how people use certain tools; your new team member might have a different cultural background that doesn't organically align with you and the rest of the team.

Where an ad hoc onboarding in a centralised organisation can count on non-verbal communication (somebody looking puzzled as they're trying to figure out how the printer works), or a social safety net of helpful team members, this is a lot harder to improvise when you are remote.

We're going ahead and assume that you've just spent a lot of time and effort finding the right person for your organisation and are planning on a long relationship with them. Making sure they are successful in their remote role is the responsibility of both of you, but only you can help them get off to a good start.

Your onboarding process is going to depend largely on the culture you've built. If you'd like to know more about that first, feel free to skip ahead to chapter 4 where we'll talk more about the culture of remote teams.

Buddies

After you reach a certain size, you might not have the time to take your new team member by the hand and explain to them how your organisation works in person. Although creating a handbook is a great idea—more about that later—you'll notice your new hire probably has some questions you didn't anticipate or needs some further clarification. Starting a new job in a remote team can be scary, especially if asking for help means either dropping the question in a public Slack channel or barging into a stranger's direct messages. Zeus forbid you have to ask your new boss!

To help people get started we introduced a simple buddy system where we team up a new team member with a more experienced one. This helps your new hire discover everything on their own, while allowing your experienced team member to fill the holes with a more realistic outlook that you might have missed because you're not in the room with them.

But most importantly it gives them a social anchor by helping them connect with at least one person in the group who they can start building a relationship with. We've seen that the bond it creates between two people is often strong and lasts far beyond the onboarding process. This is important, because aside from the right tools, handling passwords and setting expectations for working hours and availability, it onboards them on the most important point: communication. Buddies will adjust faster as they immediately adopt your company's communication style. That's also where the biggest caveat lies: your buddies can easily copy any undesirable behaviour as well.

When picking a buddy, this is one of the things that you might want to think about. Others include:

Location – you want to pick someone that can easily communicate with your new hire. That starts with being in roughly the same time zone.
Department – think about what your new hire will be doing and pick

someone that they'll be working with. This way they'll quickly learn where they can find what they need and how to perform their tasks.

Personality – not everyone will be a good buddy. Think about who is helpful, friendly, represents your culture and is someone that you can trust.

Diversity – this can be an opportunity to match people who would otherwise not meet very often. You can decide to turn the above around and pick someone from a different department altogether, so they'll learn to see the world through their eyes. This can be especially useful if the new hire is in a different place in the chain of command. Also think about mixing culture, background, and personality.

While reading this section you might already have someone in mind, but we urge you to challenge your gut feeling. It's easy—especially for men—to unconsciously typecast specific people in this role. Women especially are too often pushed towards extracurricular caretaking unrelated to their job description. The simple practice of keeping track of who you're asking can already help you be more impartial.

After the onboarding process, you can schedule a quick review with the assigned buddy to get their perspective on the new hire and make sure you didn't miss any character flaws. This lets you review both the success of your hiring and onboarding process by getting a second opinion from someone who's already part of the team.

Handbook

Another essential part of the onboarding process is an online available employee handbook. Similar to how most tech companies maintain an 'internal wiki,' a handbook can not only help with onboarding but also become a 'single source of truth.' This means that whenever someone is unsure where something is stored, what a process looks like, or what you agreed on should be the appropriate way to handle disputes, you can refer to the handbook.

It's for this reason that you need to think about this as less of an HR-produced static PDF but consider it a living document instead. With today's tools, it's easy to create a document and invite others to make edits as they see fit, or at least let them propose changes. Depending on the size of your organisation this might even be an absolute necessity to handle the scale of this project. Trust your team to contribute to the handbook, and not only will it save you time and improve the accuracy, it will also improve their involvement in carrying it out. Another argument we found very compelling is that your team ultimately best defines your culture and how that impacts policy.

Does that mean that everyone should be able to define all organisational guidelines? Probably not. Depending on your specific situation, you might want to consider certain sections to be off-limits—like your code of conduct, for example. You could also appoint certain people to manage the approval process. In any case, it's recommended that you start by covering the basics and let people build on that.

Google Docs, Confluence, or Gitlab can be great tools to do this; the latter even wrote a guide on how to write a handbook and based their entire onboarding process on it. At Gitlab, new hires aren't just expected to go through the entire handbook, but they've gone the extra mile by building a project management process alongside it. New hires will go through a multi-week course where they have to finish certain tasks related to the handbook.

If there are specific resources, you'd like your new hires to get familiar with, or tools they might be new to, consider setting up a range of tasks for them to promote self-learning while using the handbook. This can help you scale your remote onboarding process, especially if it's a repeatable process and you expect to be growing your team constantly.

New Tools

Although it's unlikely you'll hire someone unfamiliar with Slack, Google Docs, and the rest of the online tool stack—or unable to quickly adapt to it— you might want to help people get familiar with these tools. This could be done through their buddies, a special Slack channel where people could share tips, or the employee handbook. For most tools, however, you can assume some person on YouTube is doing a better job explaining it than you can. As a matter of fact, consider embedding helpful content straight in there.

If you have decided to use digital currencies to pay your team, make sure you take the time to help them understand the ramifications of this. Do they have secure access to their accounts? Do they have a backup? And most importantly, are they aware of the risks of being their own bank?

Security

A small note about security. Since you're going to be working with people that you've met on the internet, it is important to keep in mind that your legal jurisdiction might be limited. It goes without saying that you should get legal counsel, and make sure to send your team members an NDA with specific agreements about handling data and security. But aside from that, make sure that you set up an infrastructure that allows you to limit access to people until you feel comfortable trusting them, and revoke it when you stop working with them. This also applies to your communication channels, like Slack. Slack allows you to set up private channels that are invite-only, which will limit the attendance to the people that need to be involved and prevent people from being pulled into conversations they don't need to be in. Google Admin allows you to set up different roles and organisational units to prevent the wrong people from getting access to certain parts of your organisation.

External Security

Just like traditional businesses, you need to make sure you protect yourself from scammers, phishing, and other malicious attacks; this includes your remote team. With all communication and files moving online, you need to take extra precaution as the risk and potential damages are higher. There is no doubt that people with bad intentions will see the remote work revolution as an opportunity to make some money. We would advise making sure all your team members use Two-Factor Authentication (2FA) for communication (email, Slack) and access to your files. Fortunately, most modern tools support these bank-grade security measures but be aware that they might not be switched on right away.

Using a password manager is an easy way to make sure that accounts are safe, and essential if passwords need to be shared among team members. It will also allow you to force your team to regularly update their passwords, and not use the same one more than once.

In addition to these measures, having periodical conversations or online training courses to recognise and deflect such attacks can already help mitigate the risk of this happening to you.

Social Welcome

At last, the most important part of onboarding a new hire is to take a moment and welcome them to their new team members. Whether you're using Slack or think it's more suitable to do it during a meeting, giving them a chance to introduce themselves to the rest of the team can break the ice and make them feel welcomed. Your role as manager is important in this because it's likely that your team will only stop by and say hello if you ask them to.

One way we did this is by creating a non-work channel in Slack, dedicated to new introductions. After a quick announcement to the entire team, we asked the new hires to introduce themselves by telling everyone:

- Where they live
- Something about themselves
- What they're going to be working on
-     Post a picture of themselves, their environment, or something that's important to them.

It's a simple but effective way to start conversations and make people feel welcome. If you keep the channel clean, you'll end up with a long list of introductions, making it easy for newcomers to simply scroll up and read who they'll be working with.

Words from the community

Darren Murph, Head of Remote at GitLab

Shift as much of the onboarding burden from people to documentation as you can. Write down what onboarding looks like and enable new hires to self-serve by reading documentation. Pair this person with an onboarding buddy to provide a human touch to the experience. This buddy is responsible for connecting the dots within the company, making introductions, and being a one-stop-shop for the typical new hire questions.

Darcy Boles, Director of Culture and Innovation at TaxJar

Remote onboarding can be A LOT of written info! So, it's best to ensure you have daily check-ins with your new teammate and ensure to give ample time to the individual to settle in.

PART 4: CREATING CULTURE

4.1 BUILDING A REMOTE CULTURE

Your culture can make or break your company. I'm not the first person to say that.

Now, let's add the complications of having a team across the globe, with different expectations of work culture and behaviour in each country, not to mention, that you have never met any of these people in real life . . .

These are some of the additional factors you have to manoeuvre around when you are working to build a strong culture within a remote team.

We have a low staff turnover and very few people have chosen to leave our company over the last few years. So, let's have a look at some of the ways we've found that help build a culture which allows your company to thrive!

Onboarding

To follow on from the last section, onboarding is crucial for any business, but in a remote business, you are going to need your team to act autonomously from the get-go. This means the first couple of weeks it's your time to get your new team member up to speed.

Back in the early days of our business, I'll be honest, we were pretty terrible at this part of the hiring process. We would just bring people in, assign them to a project and expect them to start executing. In a few rare cases that happened. But it's not as simple as in an office environment where you can sit someone at a desk with the rest of their team and then a lot of things happen organically. You actually have to introduce your new team member to the person they report to, to all of their other teammates, really explain what each person is doing and their part in the process. If your new hire doesn't have a good grasp of this in the first week or two, you risk them falling behind. In an office environment, that team member can go for coffee with people, lunch, and sit next to different people. It's often a much smoother transition.

You can read more about onboarding in the previous chapter.

Non-work Communication Channels

Everyone needs a place to come together. In an office, this might be a kitchen, coffee area or canteen, or even somewhere down the road for lunch. That's clearly not an option here, so we have our "Watercooler" video conferencing room and "non-work" chat room in Slack.
Both of these are designed for people to meet up and hang out. People can talk about whatever they want in our non-work channel (as long as it's not offensive). We share memes, funny social media posts, wish people happy birthdays, talk about people's vacations, whatever really, there are no real rules! This is a great way for people to be able to express themselves and have some fun in a virtual environment. Same applies to our special video conference room, it's not designed for work—we have other rooms for that.

People need an outlet and a way to bond, so let them have it.

News Channel

On top of our non-work chat channels, we also have a news channel. This a place for people to share links to blog posts, news articles, podcasts, videos, anything they feel like sharing. Ours is a mix of industry-related and more general posting, I don't think there's a right and wrong way to do this. But we just try to have two channels and keep our chat as a chat, and give people another place to post content links—otherwise, everything gets a little clogged up. Again, this helps create culture because it gives people things to talk about, give alternate opinions and share what they have been viewing.

Create Teams

If you are just a few people, then that is your team. But we grew to 50 people and it just became totally unruly to really have a connection with everyone. So, we have two different types of teams.

The first is obvious. Teams divided by business function, the marketing team, the product team, etc. Nothing new there. But the second thing we did was to create social teams. We had one of our senior team as a team lead and then 6-8 people in their team.

The purpose of this team is not completely work-related. It's simply to give everyone a manager they can report to about things not related to their day-to-day tasks. We use these teams to help manage vacations, sickness, but the most important function is we set regular challenges, competitions, and games. Some of these have included, rebranding our company, pitching new business ideas, or completing challenges set by people in our network.

We've found this to be a great bonding exercise. It means that everyone also has a 'social team' they can be a part of, have regular calls with and they are part of something beyond their project teams. It's also then easier to spot if there's a problem because the sub-team leader is in charge of this.

Daily Calls

In a co-located company, there's probably a high chance that everyone has at least one meeting a day. Like or loathe meetings, they are a way to bring people together and get everyone on the same page. They are also in some respects a social event that gives a team member some time away from the rest of their tasks and to be in an environment with others.

In a remote team, I think it's essential that everyone should be on at least one call a day. That human connection, hearing people's voices or seeing someone on a conference call, it's important. Especially for people who live alone or in a truly 'remote' location. Simply put, it's good to interact with people. Even if you are the most introverted person out there, you will still want to communicate with a human after a while of not doing it.

A daily standup meeting is a minimum in my opinion and most of our team also partake in numerous other calls with project teams, clients, and other semi-regular social calls we put together. It's also a chance for everyone to talk to other members of the team or set up further calls or conversations. You can check out our chapter on meetings for more information on this.

Be clear with what you expect

Are you a strong proponent of work/life balance? Do you want people to clock in and clock out? Is your focus output not time spent?

Whatever is important to you, communicate it. This defines your culture and means it's easy to understand what you expect from your team. Make it clear!

Personally, the KPI I care about most is happy clients and tasks getting done. If someone is somehow secretly doing that in two hours a day, then good on them. Obviously, that's not ideal, but my focus is 100% on output and if people deliver, I don't bother them.

People want Autonomy

This might not be true of everyone, but my opinion is that if someone has put themselves out there and has become a remote worker (maybe with a team in a completely different part of the world) then they are confident they can operate autonomously.

My team is a complete mix of people and ages. But the one trait across all of them is their willingness and ability to work autonomously. I love it when I don't speak to someone properly for two to three days and it turns out they did everything we discussed and more.

This isn't necessarily something that can happen on day one, but let people fly, and help them when they ask for it. This is probably true of any company but in a remote team, it's the way it has to be. The nature of remote workers is to do things their way and if you let them, you'll have a happy team.

Don't Micromanage

Again, this is probably a good tip for any leader. But I'll tell you why it's more important in a remote team.

If you try to micromanage people across ten time zones you and your company will fall apart. It can be hard to not get involved, but it's just not possible to be awake at all times of the day. Once you learn to let go, you get all of that time back. I'm definitely not perfect and whenever I do end up micromanaging something, again I quickly realise that it's slowing up the whole process. When your team knows that you trust them, then there's a culture of autonomous humans who are left to get on with their jobs and are happy that they don't have someone breathing down their neck.

Monitor Happiness

This sounds stupid, right? What measuring device are we supposed to use? Well, it doesn't necessarily need a numerical value. What I'm saying is, make sure you are thinking about it and checking in on it.

For a long time, we did weekly feedback surveys that were mandatory to fill out, people could leave their feedback good and bad. We would check over them and have calls with the team if there was anything that needed a call. This was a great v1 and helped us better understand how people were feeling in the private environment of a survey.

However, as we grew, we decided to change things up and we brought in three different initiatives. We hired a Happiness Officer, which in some respects had an overlap with some of the tasks you might expect an HR person to do. The job of a Happiness Officer is to keep track of everyone and check in with everyone on a regular basis. Alongside that, coming up with fun games, tasks, calls and other activities that help ease stress, promote team culture, and give someone a person to talk to that is detached from a boss/employee relationship.

The second idea we brought in has been quarterly AMAs (ask me anything). This involves us creating a form where people can submit anonymous questions. The questions can be about anything and as long as they are professional, I answer them on a video conference call in real-time. This may sound daunting, but I don't feel I've got anything to hide from my team. So far we've done a few and I think both myself and the team have found them very valuable. They know the truth about what's going on in the company and I believe that helps the culture.

And the third concept is similar to the second. We ask a few open-ended questions and allow people to submit anonymous answers. They can write as much or little as they want and then we go through them. If there are any major talking points, then we address them. Similar to the AMA, it's a great way to find out what people are REALLY thinking and it's super valuable. If everybody is criticising the same thing then we can address that, tell people we are addressing it and it creates a cycle of trust, which ultimately benefits the culture of the business.

Bringing in these three initiatives has allowed us to have a much stronger grasp of whether our team is happy or frustrated, it also allows us to nip problems in the bud before they blossom into catastrophic issues.

Be Flexible

Building a strong company culture is to learn to be flexible. Running a company across the globe, different times of day for everyone, different home situations, family obligations, internet speeds and working hour preferences. The reality is, you just have to be flexible and accept that things don't always go to plan.

Maybe you have an important call but one of your team members has to take their children to school. Maybe it's an important religious festival that day. Maybe there's been a major storm and their internet got wiped out. Yes, I've experienced all of these.

Sometimes in a remote team, things are just out of people's control and life happens. Don't punish people for that. If it's something that happens over and over, then you may have a point. But otherwise, if someone misses a call because their internet is down and they have notified you, then you just have to deal with it and understand that it might not be their fault. When you are all in one office, part of the reason for being in that office is to mitigate many of these obstacles. But you can't always do that with a truly global remote team; no two countries and setups are the same.

Invest in your team

And this brings me to my last point, invest in your team. This actually means many things.

If you have the budget, help your team out where you can. Can you help them with higher speed internet, a new laptop, a camera or mic, some other perks for their home office?

Are you giving your team an adequate vacation allowance? We give all of our team globally the same vacation days we get in Germany (20 days), even though we don't technically have to. Do you promise to cover sick days? Can you help cover a team member's health insurance? Will you fly your team to meet each other once or twice a year?

All of these are important questions to answer. We do as much of this as we can afford. It's important to invest in your team, they will reward you with their efforts. Don't treat people differently just because you can, and the laws allow you to.

If someone is early in their career, it's a big responsibility to help them craft a plan. We work in a niche, new area, and so part of the task here is to show how to develop their own path, without going blindly.

I hope you found this to be a useful starting point. There are maybe many more nuanced areas we have not covered, but broadly speaking if you follow the above steps you should have a happy, functioning remote culture that's more powerful than anything else for your success.

◆ ◆ ◆

Words from the community

Darren Murph, Head of Remote at GitLab

Building a culture across a company where there are no offices requires intentionality. While technology and tools are enabling companies to operate efficiently in a remote setting, it's important to focus on documenting culture first, then using tools to support.

In co-located companies, it's easy to let culture be shaped by office decor, the neighbourhood in which a company's headquarters is located, or the loudest voice in the room. Not only is this dangerous—one's culture can oscillate based on external factors—but it's not a usable strategy in a remote environment.

In a remote team, there's no office vibe, hip coffee, or Spotify playlists that decide the culture, which is a gift. Instead, culture is written down. Culture is equal to the values you write down, and what you do as a leadership team to reinforce those values.

Darcy Boles, Director of Culture and Innovation at TaxJar

It's ALL about fostering connection. Culture happens naturally for about the first 20 employees, and then it's essential that companies have one person dedicated to fostering the scale of it.

You don't have water coolers or hallways to bump into one another so it's a great idea to ensure you create interest-specific channels to help individuals connect on a personal level. We love our Pets at TaxJar channel as well as a Foodie channel and Kids of Taxjar!

Culture also isn't just the fun stuff, culture is your operating system, it's how you communicate with one another, the language and style of comms that you expect, the hours expected to work etc.—it's essential to get clear on these and your values and model it from the inside out.

4.2 CONFLICT RESOLUTION

"Conflict can and should be handled constructively; when it is, relationships benefit. Conflict avoidance is not the hallmark of a good relationship. On the contrary, it is a symptom of serious problems and of poor communication." **–Harriet B. Braiker**

We've all been there. The dreaded office conflict between two or more employees. It causes stress, divides teams, and can lead to delays in delivering your product and/or service.

But how do you mitigate when a conflict exists in a digital space?

Dealing with conflicts in a remote team setting requires a streamlined solution that can take time to identify. For myself, the following areas of focus have been effective in helping me resolve the majority of disputes, arguments, or troubles in a remote team setting.

Conflicts that occur in digital communication channels like Slack, Discord, Teams, and so many others are inherently slippery. People can say anything they want, messages can be edited and/or deleted, and there's the ever-present feeling that *it's not really tangible.* This of course, as you can imagine, is not the complete truth. Who hasn't been negatively affected by a text message or email before?

People still get frustrated, arguments occur, and disputes can elevate without proper intervention. For that reason, in my own experience, I try to take what is written as gospel, because at the end of the day, it is one of the few metrics we have to base our emotions off of.

Determining the root cause

Personal vs. Business

One of the things I've had to work on over time is understanding if a dispute between two employees is stemming from something personal, or from a more practical business reason. Of course, you can have both of these in the mix, but it's often clear when something is more heavily weighing on one or the other.

It's important to identify which because it will lead to how you resolve the conflict. Personal issues between two team members often stem from past disputes, a sort of "build-up" until they turn vocal, or in our case, texted! It's important to identify a) each team member's personality and b) how they've conducted themselves in past conflicts. These two observations should allow you to weigh more heavily on one or the other for understanding because ultimately, you do want a 50/50 agreement.

For example, let's say the dispute between two team members is focused on a business issue neither party can agree on. Let's go with the topic of email marketing. One believes it should be done using option A, the other option B. The first step is to visit your company's documentation. Use any paperwork, digital notebooks, or google docs you have that clarify a direction to move forward in. The team member who proposes a new, and ultimately "different" solution may actually be right (even if it differs from the documentation), but those types of changes can't be decided in a heated moment. It's best to re-group at a later time and go over why that person's opinion may, in fact, be a stronger solution for your company. Stick to the facts!

Remember, your goal is to settle and cool down a heated moment, letting both parties know you are hearing them out and will re-group to discuss the business matter in more detail at a later time.

Finding Solutions

Build & reciprocate trust

It's not just about creating a space where conflicts are solved, but one where they can be shared without fear of repercussion.

Communication between managers and employees is best when there's a space to be heard. In fact, trust has to be earned. How do you do that? How do you encourage your team to come forward and express their daily conflicts? What if they're not happy with something that you did?

You need to foster that trust so that everyone can share their thoughts to each other. It's easy to keep it bottled up in a remote setting because you don't have to see people, which means you can hide behind the black mirror. I encourage all leaders to communicate with their team as frequently as possible about how they are doing both in work and outside of work. Everyone wants to be heard and showing you care can make the world of difference.

Assume positive intent

Those of us now thrust into the world of remote work will no doubt have experienced that pang of defensiveness when we get a curt answer via online chat.

Whether it's a "yes", "np" or "right." We read into it as a sign of disagreement, rejection, or just plain rudeness. But we don't know if that person is in a rush to get on the next call, dealing with a screaming kid, or if it's simply the way they communicate. When you can't see someone's facial expressions or body language, it's easy to misinterpret, and we tend to jump to conclusions and assume it's about us.

In *This is Water*, David Foster Wallace spoke of how we've been hardwired to be self-centred, and so we all see the world through our own "lens of self." But we can change how we look at things, and instead assume the best instead of the worst. So, my tip is to consciously practise empathy first and give the benefit of the doubt. This approach is called API: assume positive intent.

Making it Real

So, what do you do when things cannot be solved through straightforward intervention? Our best advice, and what has worked countless times for us, is to get both parties (and yourself, the "interventionist") on a conference call. This will make things much more tactile and less slippery for your disputed parties—levelling the playing field so to speak. It is drastically more difficult to convey heated opinions when you have to face someone else's voice.

More Drastic Measures

What if your team members just can't get things resolved? In this case, we recommend trying to move them to different focus areas, whether it be to look at engaging with different clients or working on different tasks that don't overlap. It doesn't have to be permanent, but sometimes people need that space (yes, even in the digital world) to recompose themselves and come back to their counterparts with a fresh perspective.

Again, as mentioned earlier, many conflicts occur because of an existing personal disagreement between two individuals. It's hard to change who we are, but it's well worth it for everyone involved to really identify *what* the issue is, and work towards solving that first. If it's something that can be solved with time apart, then so be it. But you have to try everything possible.

Prevention

Better yet—learn to anticipate potential issues. When onboarding new team members provide some training on communication in the remote setting.

Resolutions

Over the years working on a remote team, I've found that most conflicts end up with three types of resolutions.

The win-win

In this resolution, both sides of the discussion will walk away with something to work on, feeling as if they've been heard throughout the conversation.

The win-lose

Less desirable but still successful, two employees converge to discuss a dispute but only one is left with a satisfactory solution. The other may understand the reasoning for this outcome, but they still feel they did not get what they wanted. Although unfortunate, many discussions end this way because ultimately, some problems can not satisfy both sides of the argument.

The lose-lose

A tough pill to swallow, and one which doesn't occur as frequently, but this is where neither party gets what they want. When this type of scenario comes to light, it's more important than ever to make it clear that hope is not lost. Emphasize that the communication that occurred led to a resolution where both parties have something to think about. I suggest even pencilling a follow-up meeting with both sides and letting them know that some time away from the topic can bring new items to light.

As leaders, we're constantly hurdling over financial, product, service, personal, and countless other issues on a daily basis. It's natural to want to avoid conflicts between employees because it can feel like a waste of time. No one enjoys having to resolve conflicts between team members, but it's part of the job. So, remember, focus on empathy, listening, and creating a space where people can share what they're going through. If you do this well, you're off to a great start already.

◆ ◆ ◆

Words from the community

Darcy Boles, Director of Culture and Innovation at TaxJar

Over, over, over-communicate! If something could even slightly be taken the wrong way in written form, hop on a Zoom call, hash it out then and there. Remote communication can easily turn into a terrible game of telephone if you don't have standards of communication and the ability to talk about the hard stuff. 1:1s are essential, as well as consistent feedback and two-way communication.

John Eckman, CEO of 10up

Conflict resolution is a challenge in any professional services / agency setting. I'm a big believer that management doesn't eliminate conflict but provides healthy channels for its expression and resolution. In a distributed company that means really doubling down on active listening and empathy, as well as providing clear escalation paths for the times when a team or set of individuals can't resolve their issues themselves.

I've found the book 'The Four Agreements' incredibly useful. It comes out of the "self-help" space, and the first chapter in particular can be hard for some people to take as it is very "new age / spiritual." If you skip that chapter and just dive into the four agreements themselves, however, the advice works very well to drive successful interpersonal cooperation and collaboration. (I've given some talks on this subject using the book as a framework).

At the end of the day, even though much of what we do is incredibly complicated technically, it's the human and interpersonal issues that are truly the most challenging.

4.3 INCENTIVES AND EVENTS

Another part of building a strong remote culture is through incentives and team events. We've noticed that in overcoming the challenges of being remote, team motivation can be a powerful asset, so using these tools to build on that is worth dedicating some thought.

Although the objective of your organisation is probably clear, you want to make sure there's ample time for extracurricular activities so the team can get to know each other, build a relationship that will enable trust, and help foster an internal system for support. Many books have already been dedicated to why this is important, so we won't digress further.

We decided to write about both incentives and events because they both share a single intention; it's a conscious dedication to invest in the culture of your team. Incentives are the carrot for your team. A way to guide them in the right direction and reinforce positive behaviour. They signal that you recognise their efforts and appreciate what they're doing.

Events do that too, albeit in a more ambiguous way. But on top of that, they are an excuse to stop what everyone's doing and reflect on what you've accomplished, or perhaps introduce some play. They signal that you care about your team and their wellbeing and growth, as much as your organisational objective. Whether you're taking a short moment to celebrate success, or a couple of days to organise a hackathon, events are a great practice to work on the relationship with your remote team.

Aside from motivating people and giving your team a fun break from work, events also help to:

- Promote teamwork
- Spark creativity

- Learn new skills
- Improve interpersonal skills

You'll notice from looking at that list that there's a lot of different directions you can go in. We certainly haven't explored all options, and it's by no means a checklist that should be all-encompassing. If anything, that connects all of our events, it is that they should be fun.

When planning events, we're making the distinction between two types:

- Celebrations
- Activities

Not all celebrations and activities need to be elaborate; we try to remember birthdays and invite everyone to help make the birthday person feel special on their day. This can just be as simple as a message in a public Slack channel, for example. If you've built the right team and nurture a fun and supportive culture, people will jump in with kind words, emojis, and the occasional GIF. Sometimes we spontaneously launch a challenge, like creating the funniest or most original holiday-themed profile picture or solve a puzzle that will be the start of an announcement. You can attach a financial or symbolic prize to them; mostly, people just enjoy the communal activity.

Celebrations

Since you might be working with people from different cultures, consider that not everybody will celebrate something during the December holiday period. Although that doesn't need to stop you from celebrating during that month (it is after all the end of the year as well), why not also take a moment to observe Eid or Chinese New Year?

Celebrating success also deserves some extra attention in remote teams. Not everyone will be involved in every aspect of your organisation, so make the extra effort to include the rest in your organisation's success. It's easy for a sales department to announce a new contract in their Slack channel, or for the marketing team to discuss their performance in an internal meeting without ever reaching the rest of the organisation. We know this happens in centralised organisations as well, but the risk of information being siloed is larger in remote teams. It's your job to be conscious of this and regularly celebrate success with the entire organisation.

Your biggest challenge with celebrating events is going to be overcoming time zones. For our holiday party, we've picked a time that would have Australians drinking beer and Canadians drinking coffee; in Europe and Africa, they were somewhere between both. Depending on your team, you might want to involve them in how you're planning the celebration. We tried hosting regular pizza parties and even a book club, but ultimately people decided that the timing made this difficult; it turned out that this was mostly fun for people at the end of their workday.

The one annual tradition we never miss is Secret Santa. Since our first December as a remote team we ask everyone to take the (next) day off, so they can join in at the same time as we review our year, play games, give everyone a holiday gift (more about this in the next chapter) and have a bit of fun. For the people who have never heard of Secret Santa: everyone agrees to buy a small gift for one of their co-workers that is being randomly assigned to them. We keep it a secret who gave the gift, to then let people vote on the most original gift. This is a fun way to let your team participate in the creative process of running a remote team, as they figure out what you can give someone who lives in a different continent. We've seen inventive gifts and even more inventive ways to present them, like a custom website to explain what it is, or a cryptographic puzzle.

Make sure you prepare for a couple of fun activities as well as some fillers while you wait for people to join, or in case anything goes wrong. We usually collect fun trivia about the organisation and strange facts about team members, and use Kahoot to let people participate from their phones. In between rounds, we asked people to describe their country in 5 emojis, give us a tour around their house, and post the last picture they took with their phone. Each of those should spin off some interesting conversations. However fun this is, you're probably dealing with different time zones, so you want to limit your events to two, or three hours max.

Another initiative we really enjoyed came from our Happiness Officer. Every other week they would pick a different person on our team to give a little extra attention to. This could be anyone, from a part-time newbie to a core team member (though you should exclude the leadership). At the end of a biweekly happiness call to check in how everyone is doing, they'd announce the coming 7 days would be marked 'Olga Week', or 'Daniel Week'. During this time, the entire team is asked to proactively help the person out in any way and make it a fun couple of days. It might sound silly, but as the rest of the team joined in on celebrating the individual by posting memes, YouTube links to Daniel-themed songs, and helping them out, we've experienced a noticeable uptake on morale and team spirit. You shouldn't be afraid to try new things that might seem odd in a traditional office environment. It's fun to experiment.

Some things to keep in mind when you're planning your event:

- Include your team in picking a time
- Larger teams could use a host
- Make sure you're entire team fits inside your video conference
- Include games about your industry or company
- Let the fun continue in your Slack or other communication tool

Activities

Another way to look at events is to organise specific activities. This doesn't need to be framed by a meeting or an occasion and can last just an hour or be ongoing. What sets them apart from celebrations is that they're likely to be more closely tied to incentives. We've used activities to challenge our team to work together or embark on a creative quest by themselves. The goal is to both have fun and spark some competition.

Whether you decide to plan something ahead of time, introduce a new recurring challenge, or just had a spontaneous idea; activities can really break the mould. It helped us get through some stressful times and has even been a good education tool.

We like making a little competition out of everything to keep people engaged. So, when we noticed our Slack looked a little dull, we ran a spontaneous competition and asked everyone to upload a new custom emoji. People could react to that message with their emoji and the one with the most usage would win a small prize.

We realised that though this was fun, a couple of people felt left out as they were either just about to have dinner or didn't have their coffee yet. Make sure you pick an as-neutral-as-possible time and give people a heads-up.

Other activities that have worked out well are the ones that spark creativity. After a period of growth with a lot of new people, we knew we should invest in team building, and were also looking for ways to train everyone new skills. We divided the team up in groups of 10 people and gave them a monthly task. This ranged from presenting what they considered to be our internal values to small marketing challenges. For the latter, we asked friends in other organisations to send us a short video introducing everyone to the next challenge. Not only did this push our team to work with people from different departments and promote a bit of competition, but it was also a great opportunity for them to practise creative thinking. At the end of each challenge, we awarded points for the best performance and execution.

Real-Life Events

One thing that we didn't really discuss is the notion of bringing the team together in real life. It probably goes without saying, but you should try to get the whole team together concerning budget, immigration offices, and lifestyle permits. We have made an effort to plan an event at least once a year for the entire organisation. Start your planning way ahead of time and especially think of the travel restrictions some people might have to deal with. We once spent weeks trying to coordinate Japan's visa requirements for one of our key team members only to hit a wall at the very end.

If for whatever reason meeting up with your entire team is not an option, you should at least try to meet most of them yourself. We've been able to leverage conferences all over the world to fly in the people that are close enough, able, and willing. You can certainly build a team without ever meeting them, but the value you'll get from sharing a drink with them in person is worth every penny. How to properly navigate the initial awkward phase of knowing someone very well but only meeting them for the first time however, we still do not know.

Incentives

Described as the carrot earlier, incentives can indeed be a healthy snack to motivate your team. Whether you tie them to objectives, use them to reinforce behaviour, or connect them to activities; incentives are an easy way to motivate people. There's a caveat though: rewards don't always work well when there's already plenty of intrinsic motivation. This means that a driven team might not need a reward or can even feel a little 'cheap' for doing the work for an extra handout. You should also be aware that incentives can pit people against each other. We got some complaints from the losing side after one of our activities because they felt they hadn't been scored fairly. The prize? We hadn't even announced one yet.

Aside from picking the right incentives, you should think about what you expect from offering the incentive in the first place. Author Daniel Pink, and plenty more, have written about the science behind what drives us, so we won't get into that topic too much.

There are a few things we've learned about offering incentives in a remote environment, though. First, it's helpful if you can define clear rules and measurable results when engaging in competitions. If you're transparent about how people can compete and win, chances are that everyone will consider it fair play. The second observation is that it helps to make people part of the process. When we picked our organisation's values, we let each group vote on their favourite values from other teams and picked the top three values, purposes, and purpose. Transparency is the best way to deal with opposition.

Another consideration is to see your incentive as an encouragement. Our 'person-week' was not so much an incentive as everyone knew it would be their turn eventually, but it did motivate people in anticipation of their own 'week.' People like to win, even if the reward is just a moment of attention and recognition from your team. To make sure your incentive actually encourages people, it's your responsibility to make sure they feel like they have a shot.

Which brings us to the downside of voting. We started noticing a pattern when we asked people to vote on The Executor of the Month; a cash bonus for the person that got the most done in the eyes of their team. This wasn't about measurable results, but purely a vote on who deserves it. The problem was that after a few months the nomination seemed to rotate between a few of the usual suspects. Granted, they worked hard and certainly deserved it, but it started to weigh on the other people in the team. Not just because their efforts didn't seem to be enough, but because they too recognised it had become a popularity contest, and they weren't winning.

We decided to add our veto to the process, and to also add The Asteroid of the Month (for biggest impact) and later The Motivator of the Month (for helping other people and their positive impact on the culture) to even it out and make sure we have plenty of rotation.

4.4 GIFTS AND BONUSES

When you want to motivate your remote team by giving them something extra, you're hit with a couple of operational challenges. When we were discussing our options for sending everyone a little something extra at the end of the year, we found ourselves shooting down idea after idea. We came up with a bunch of funny designs for team sweaters, but soon realised that printing them in one location and then shipping each one to a different address wouldn't only be a huge headache, it would also mean we'd be spending more money on shipping than on the actual gift. We considered printing on location but finding 20 companies in other countries where we didn't speak the language would've been a full-time job.

Despite borderless economies and cloud-based communication tools, you're going to run into the limitations of being in different countries eventually. Of course, most of the issues can be overcome if you have enough resources as it's ultimately a question of scale and dedication. But until then, let's look into your options when it comes to giving your team a little something special.

Home Office Gifts

As we discussed in part 2, one of the decisions you need to make when putting together a remote team is where you want people to work from. You can expect most people to work from home from either a dedicated home office or their living room, though some people prefer to work from their favourite co-working space. We even worked with people who decided to take their work with them on the road as they travelled. In either case, your team is probably not going to end up in a well-groomed work environment as was traditionally the case. The benefit is that everyone can get their preferred equipment and setup, but as the transition to working from home isn't always a conscious one, you might want to consider helping them improve their space.

Some things you can think about getting your team to improve their home office:

- Plants
- Smart speakers
- Headphones and webcam
- Laptop stand and keyboard
- Standing desk
- Desk chair

You might notice that many of these items fall under the category 'standard office equipment.' Depending on your policy, you might have already purchased this for them or communicated that you expect them to invest in their own home office. In that case, think about how you can add extras, like a plant, to make their office a little more fun.

Digital Gifts

Having read the previous pages, however, you probably see why the ideas above might pose an issue. Unless you and your organisation ships desk chairs all over the world for a living, digital gifts will be a better option.

Depending on your geographical distribution, though, even with digital gifts it can be really hard to come up with something that will work for everyone in each country. We've looked at Spotify, Netflix, Blinkist, Amazon— surprisingly none of them were available in *all* countries where we have people. Even if they are, you will often find that the service is tied to the country of your credit card, and that ordering gift cards for each person in each country is nearly impossible. Some websites let you buy prepaid in-store credit for these subscriptions, but that is again tied to the country they operate in. If all of that isn't complicated enough, your team might already have a subscription for one or a bunch of these services.

Cash Bonuses & Reimbursements

The solution to these problems is about as thoughtful as giving someone money on Christmas Eve: you let them buy their own gifts. It was never our first choice, but as we considered our options, we realised that everyone will be happiest if they can choose their own gift and we reimburse them for it. This is also better than just giving people a cash bonus, as you can make sure they actually buy something meaningful instead of it disappearing in their bank account. We set up a Google Form for people to tell us what they planned to buy, and asked them to send us their receipts for reimbursement later. This also works for home office gifts or any other physical items.

When it comes to incentivising people or rewarding them for participating in an activity, a cash bonus might make a little more sense. We decided to buy people something nice for their home office, like a nice plant or new speaker, after they won our Motivator of the Month award, but gave them a cash bonus for reaching a certain performance goal. You can balance your decision based on how competitive people might get, or how much effort you expect they'll have to put into the challenge. If you're using cryptocurrency to pay your team, you don't need to wait until the end of the month, and you can pay out bonuses or reimbursements instantly.

Whatever the occasion is, think about your team and what would work for them; logistically and thematically. And remember that some people might not have what you want to offer in their country. If you're still looking for ideas, here's a couple of things we considered for remote gifts:

- Spotify or Apple Music subscription
- Amazon Prime
- Audible subscription
- Blinkist Books
- Netflix subscription
- eReader
- Local gym subscription

CONCLUSION

We hope you've enjoyed this practical guide to running a remote team. There is a strong tailwind behind the concept of remote work and in the not too distant future, this book could become common knowledge. We would love to see that happen and we hope that in the meantime all of you founders, entrepreneurs, managers and leaders have learned something that will improve your day-to-day.

When we started building our remote team, we found it quite difficult to get this kind of information and there were definitely a lot fewer articles about this topic, even a few years ago. We hope that any knowledge we have gained from our experience managing a remote team of 50 has now been passed onto you and you go out there and do the same!

Remote teams are about more than just working from home or hiring someone in another state. It means hiring, communicating, and collaborating completely online and doing this on a global scale. There are nearly three billion people online globally and any of them might have the ability to be your next hire. Be open, be honest, be welcoming. You will find some incredible people out there that you could have never expected to meet.

With today's connectivity, cloud-based tools, and an English-speaking generation that grew up communicating online, your options are nearly limitless when hiring globally. This is an unprecedented age of education and opportunity, which are the perfect conditions for growing a company.

Use time zones to your advantage, learn how to collaborate online and start building your business. No need for commuting or moving people halfway across the globe for a job. Discover what it means to build a remote culture; make time to talk to people, maybe even try to meet them in person at some point. It's worth the investment.

Above anything, there is nothing more important than TRUST. Civilised human society over the last 5,000 years has been built on it. Remember to put people first and create an environment you would want to work in yourself.

What's Next for Remote Teams?

As you may have noticed, this book focuses very much on the here and now. For us, a remote team is about the right now and these are the tools, tactics, and methods we used to wrangle an army of distributed workers. However, we are very aware that these environments change quickly.

There could be huge paradigm shifts in society over the coming decades that alter our urban environments and subsequently our economies. What is the future of commercial office space? Will people migrate to warmer climes with nothing but a laptop? Will we see the new rise of suburbia? What will change about education or childcare? What are the implications of all of this on taxes, pensions, and healthcare systems? How will workers' rights be protected across borders?

We don't exactly know right now, but we are exploring all of these issues and more with our second organisation dGen, a think tank based here with us in Berlin. dGen stands for Decentralised Generation, which is our term for the next generation after Gen Z, who will be 18 years old between 2030 and 2045.

By 2030, the world could look very different, so we are focused on writing research reports that look at the impact of emerging technology on this future generation. The future of work is an important topic for us, and you'll be able to find our report examining some of the implications on dgen.org

Thank you for making it this far into our book. We hope that we've helped inspire you to go out there and do this for yourself.